KNOWLEDGE OF THE HIGHER WORLDS
HOW IS IT ACHIEVED?

RUDOLF STEINER

KNOWLEDGE OF THE HIGHER WORLDS HOW IS IT ACHIEVED?

Revised translation by D.S.O. and C.D.

Rudolf Steiner Press
London

Revised and enlarged edition of
The Way of Initiation with *Initiation
and its Results*, 1923. Translated by
G. Metaxa
Reprinted 1928, 1932, 1934
Third English edition, 1927. Trans-
lated by G. Metaxa
Reprinted 1938, 1942, 1944, 1947
Fourth English edition, 1958. Revised
by M. Cotterell
Fifth English edition, revised, 1963
Sixth English edition, 1969. Revised
by D. S. O. and C. D.
Sixth edition, second impression, 1973

The volume in the Complete Edition of Rudolf Steiner's works
containing the text from which the translation has been made
and revised is entitled: *Wie erlangt man Erkenntnisse der höheren
Welten?* 20th edition. (No. 10 in the *Bibliographical Survey*, 1961.)
This English edition is published by permission of the *Rudolf
Steiner Nachlassverwaltung*, Dornach, Switzerland.

S.B.N. 85440 220 9 hardback
85440 221 7 paperback

MADE AND PRINTED IN GREAT BRITAIN BY
THE GARDEN CITY PRESS LIMITED
LETCHWORTH, HERTFORDSHIRE SG6 1JS

CONTENTS

FOREWORD TO 1969 EDITION

More than fifty years ago Rudolf Steiner foretold that during the course of the century there would arise in mankind a great need for forms of experience other than and beyond those given by the intellectual logical mind. Our progenitors from the time of Descartes and Bacon, Locke and Newton, believed that they had at last discovered a form of cognition which would release them from the limitations of the past and lead to a full and true knowledge of man and the universe. Today more and more people are experiencing this form of cognition not as a release but a barrier. Side by side with the explorations of outer space there has arisen a longing for spiritual exploration based on the release of deeper powers of the mind and soul. It is true that this exploration often takes facile and even grotesque forms, but the fact that it is so widely present separates the second half of our century from the first perhaps more deeply than all the technical achievements which (on the date of writing this introduction) have placed the first men on the moon.

Knowledge of the Higher Worlds, therefore, is a book which—like so many of the achievements of Rudolf Steiner—has grown more modern with the passage of the years. For two reasons it is a sure guide for modern man's spiritual exploration. Firstly, it is based on the clarity of thinking which we owe to the very forms of thought which have separated us from all direct perception of the spiritual beings behind the physical framework, or skeleton, of the universe. The aim of Steiner's method is not to deny but to extend that clear thinking beyond its present limitations. Secondly it recognises—as all genuine disciplines have always recognised—that the path to spiritual worlds is an arduous and dangerous one, calling for the utmost self-control in thought and word and deed. Man is a unity, and he cannot develop himself in his life of knowledge without a corresponding, and even greater, development in his life of feeling and will.

Hence what may be called the preliminary exercises outlined in this book are intimately concerned with the enhancement of ordinary perceptions and common virtues. You are called upon to increase your powers of observation of the world of nature, your sensitivity to everyday sights and sounds: to enter with a greater selflessness into the interests and outlook, the inner being, of your fellow men: to undertake conscious actions which you generally perform mechanically and instinctively: to silence your critical faculty and enter sympathetically into views and opinions which you might ordinarily consider intolerable or even ludicrous.

It is across the threshold of such a transformation of your daily life that you enter upon the many specific exercises recommended in this book for attaining not merely a *perception* but a *knowledge* of higher worlds. Many people today—either by some kind of inheritance, or through the natural evolution taking place in human life, or through the taking of drugs—have some kind of spiritual experiences. But they remain mere perceptions. It is only when a man takes into his direct perception of spiritual forces and beings the clarity of thinking and judgment which he can win from the proper use of modern consciousness, that he can evaluate his perceptions, can relate them to each other, and *know* what he perceives. This is a book about knowledge, not mere clairvoyant faculties.

Probably more people today have spiritual experiences than are willing to admit it—even to themselves. The age demands that such experiences be made conscious, and be transformed into knowledge, not by banal experiments with cards to prove the existence of E.S.P., but by awakening 'the faculties slumbering in every human soul'. It is the call to perfect and enhance the one instrument which—as Rudolf Steiner has pointed out—the modern natural scientist does not consider himself capable of improving—the knowledge faculty of the knower himself.

A. C. H.

21 July 1969

PREFACE TO THE EIGHTH EDITION

When I came to go through the contents of this book for the new edition, only minor alterations seemed to me to be necessary. On the other hand I have added an Appendix in which I have been at pains to speak with greater precision than before of the foundations of the life of soul upon which the communications made in the book must rest, if they are not to be misunderstood. I believe that what is said in this Appendix may be able to show many an opponent of anthroposophical Spiritual Science that his judgment had been justified only because he had imagined Spiritual Science to be something quite other than itself, while he had entirely failed to grasp what it really is.

Rudolf Steiner

May, 1918

PREFACE TO THE FIFTH EDITION

For this new edition of *Knowledge of the Higher Worlds*, the text of ten years ago has been worked through in every detail. The need for revision arises naturally in accounts of experiences of the soul and its paths of development such as are given in this book. With every part of such an account the soul of the writer remains intimately connected, and in every part there is something which works continually upon his soul. It was almost inevitable, therefore, that this activity of soul should be bound up with an endeavour to improve the clarity and definition of the earlier presentation.

Here is the origin of what I have tried to do for the present new edition. All essential features, all fundamental themes, remain as they were; but there are some important changes. In many passages I have been able to achieve greater precision in characterising details. This seemed to me important. If anyone wishes to apply in his own soul-life what is communicated in this book, he needs to be able to grasp the nature of the path of development described, with the greatest possible exactitude. Misunderstandings are far more apt to arise with descriptions of inner, spiritual processes than with descriptions of the physical world. They are made possible by many factors: the mobility inherent in the life of soul, the necessity never to forget how different this life of soul is from life in the physical world, and much else. In this new edition I have made a point of identifying those parts of the book where such misunderstandings may arise and have tried to forestall them by redrafting the passages in question.

When I wrote the articles of which the book is comprised, many things had to be put differently from what is possible today, when for the last ten years facts based on knowledge of higher worlds have been published. In my books, *Occult Science—an Outline*, *The Spiritual Guidance of Man and of Mankind*, *A Road to Self-Knowledge*, particularly in *The Threshold of the Spiritual World*, and in other writings, spiritual processes are described whose existence it was necessary to indicate in this book more than ten years ago, but in words different from those that seem appropriate now. At that time I had to say of many things not described in the book that they could be learnt through 'oral communication'. By now, a great deal that was indicated in this way has been published. These indications, however, did not perhaps completely avert mistaken opinions on the part of readers. The *personal* relationship of an aspirant for spiritual training to this or that teacher might have been regarded as much more essential than it is. In this new edition I hope that by the way in which many details are presented, I have succeeded in emphasising more sharply that for anyone who is seeking spiritual training in accordance with present-day spiritual conditions, a *direct* relationship to the objective spiritual world is much more important than a relationship to the personality of a teacher. Even in the course of spiritual training the teacher will more and more adopt the position merely of a helper, similar to that adopted, according to modern views, in any other branch of knowledge. I believe I have sufficiently stressed that in spiritual training the teacher's authority and the pupil's faith in him should play no other rôle than that prevailing in any other domain of knowledge or of life. It seems to me that much will depend upon gaining an increasingly right judgment of this relationship of the spiritual investigator to people who become interested in the findings of his research. So I believe I have improved the book in passages where, after ten years, I could see a need for improvement.

The new edition of this book was already printed when the Great War, which mankind is now experiencing, began. And I have to write this preface while my soul is deeply stirred by these fateful events.

Rudolf Steiner

Berlin, 7 September 1914

PREFACE TO THE THIRD EDITION

The contents of this book appeared originally as a series of essays under the title: *How is Knowledge of the Higher Worlds achieved?* A work of this kind, dealing with a way of development that enables man to apprehend the supersensible worlds, should not appear in a new form without some prefatory remarks. Its communications concerning the development of the human soul are intended to meet different needs. In the first place the intention is to give some help to those who feel drawn to the findings of spiritual research and are impelled to ask: whence do those who claim to be able to say something about higher riddles of life obtain their knowledge? Spiritual Science has something to say about these riddles. Whoever wishes actually to perceive the facts leading to this claim must rise to the plane of supersensible knowledge. He must tread the path which this book attempts to describe. But it would be a mistake to suppose that the communications of Spiritual Science are valueless for anyone who has neither inclination nor opportunity to tread this path himself. In order to *investigate* the facts, a capacity to penetrate into the supersensible worlds is essential. But once they have been investigated and the findings communicated, sufficient conviction of the truth of the communications can be acquired by one who does not himself perceive the facts.

A large part of the communications can at once be put to the test by applying to them quite freely a healthy faculty of judgment—provided that this freedom is not hampered by any of the various preconceptions now so abundantly prevalent in human life. It may easily happen, for instance, that someone discovers here or there a statement which seems to him at variance with certain findings of modern science. The truth is that there is no finding of science which runs counter to the results of spiritual research. Nevertheless it is easy to believe that this or that dictum of science conflicts with communications about the higher worlds, if the scientific conclusions are not studied from every aspect and without bias. It will be found that the more open-mindedly Spiritual Science is compared with the positive achievements of modern science, the more perfectly can their full agreement be recognised.

Other statements of Spiritual Science will admittedly more or less elude a purely intellectual judgment. But those who realise that not only the intellect, but also *healthy* feeling, can be a judge of truth will be able without difficulty to come to terms with these statements also. And when this feeling is not impelled to this or that opinion by sympathy or antipathy, but, entirely unimpeded by prejudice, allows the fruits of knowledge of the spiritual worlds to work upon it, a sound judgment based on feeling will result. And there are still many other ways whereby this knowledge can be substantiated for those who cannot or do not desire to tread the path into the supersensible world. Such people can certainly feel the value of this knowledge for life even though they learn it only from the communications of spiritual investigation. Not everyone can immediately become a seer; but the seer's knowledge is healthy nourishment for everyone. Everyone can apply this knowledge in life. And whoever does so will soon realise what it can mean in all spheres of life, and what is lacking when it is rejected. When rightly applied in life, knowledge of the supersensible worlds proves not to be unpractical but practical in the highest degree.

However, if someone does not himself wish to tread the path to higher knowledge, he may, if he is drawn to the facts to be observed when it is followed, ask—How does the seer arrive at these facts? This book endeavours to give those who are interested in this question a picture of what has to be undertaken in order really to know the supersensible world. It hopes to present the path into the supersensible world in such a way that even a person who is not himself following it may gain confidence in what is said by one who has trodden it. Having become aware of how the spiritual investigator works and having accepted the validity of his method, someone may say—The impression made upon me by the account of the path into the higher worlds enables me to understand why the facts imparted here seem to me enlightening. This book may therefore prove to be of service to those who desire added strength and assurance in their sense of truth and feeling for truth with regard to the supersensible world. But the

16

book would no less like to offer something to those who are themselves seeking the path to supersensible knowledge. The truth of what is presented here will best be proven by those persons who make it reality within their own being. Whoever has this aim will do well to remind himself again and again that in any account of the soul's development more is called for than familiarity with the contents— which is often all that is attempted in the case of other works. Intimate penetration into the text is necessary; it ought to be a stipulation that one particular matter shall not be grasped only through what is said about it specifically but through much that is said about quite other things. In this way it will be realised that the core of the matter does not lie in *one* truth, but in the harmony of them all. This must be very earnestly borne in mind by those who wish to carry out the exercises. A particular exercise can be correctly understood and also correctly carried out; yet it can have a wrong effect if someone who is practising it does not add to it another exercise which resolves the one-sidedness of the first into a harmony in the soul. Whoever reads this book in such a way that reading becomes an inner experience of his own will not only familiarise himself with the contents but will also have a particular feeling at one place, a different feeling at another; and then he will recognise the *import* of one or other passage for the development of the soul. He will also discover in what form he should attempt this or that exercise, according to his particular individuality. When, as here, descriptions are given of processes which must be *experienced*, it is necessary to return repeatedly to the contents; for the conviction will arise that a satisfactory understanding of much of what is said can be reached only when it has been tried out, for then, after the attempt, certain subtleties which inevitably escaped one previously will be discerned.

Those readers who do not intend to follow the path here described will find that the book contains much that can be of use for their inner life: rules for the ordering of life, indications of how this or that apparent enigma may be explained, and so on.

And many a one who has certain experiences behind him, and has in many respects become initiated through life itself, will find satisfaction when he discovers a coherent explanation of matters of which he had been aware without connecting them—things of which he was already cognisant without perhaps having brought this knowledge to a stage where he could form a satisfactory conception of it for himself.

Rudolf Steiner

Berlin, 1909

HOW IS KNOWLEDGE OF THE HIGHER WORLDS ACHIEVED?

Conditions

In every human being there slumber faculties by means of which he can acquire for himself a knowledge of higher worlds. The Mystic, the Gnostic, the Theosophist, have always spoken of a world of soul and a world of spirit which are just as real to them as the world we can see with physical eyes and touch with physical hands. Anyone who listens to them may at every moment say to himself: that of which they speak I too can know, if I develop certain powers which today still slumber within me. It can only be a matter of how to set to work to develop such faculties. Guidance on them can be given only by those who already possess such powers. As long as a human race has existed there has always been training, in the course of which individuals possessed of the higher faculties gave guidance to those who were seeking for them. Such training is called esoteric training, and the instruction received is called esoteric or occult instruction. This designation naturally causes misunderstanding. Anyone hearing it may easily be misled into believing that those concerned with this training are a specially privileged class of people who arbitrarily withhold their knowledge from their fellow-men. He may also think that perhaps nothing of real importance lies behind such knowledge, for if it were genuine knowledge—so he is tempted to think—there would be no need to make a secret of it; it could be communicated openly and its benefits made accessible to everyone.

Those who have been initiated into the nature of occult knowledge are not in the least surprised that the uninitiated should think in this way, for the secret of Initiation can be understood only by someone who has himself experienced, up to a certain stage, this Initiation into the higher mysteries of existence. How, then—it may be asked—is an uninitiated person to develop any human interest in this so-called occult knowledge? How and why should he seek for something of whose nature he can form absolutely no idea? Such a question derives from an entirely erroneous conception of the nature of occult knowledge. There is, in truth, no difference between occult knowledge and the rest of man's knowledge and skills. This occult knowledge is no more of a secret for the average human being than writing is a secret for one who has not learnt it. And just as everyone who chooses the right way to set about it can learn to write, so can everyone who seeks for the right path become a pupil of occultism; indeed, even a teacher of it. In one respect only do the conditions here differ from those that obtain with regard to external knowledge and skills. The possibility of acquiring the art of writing may be withheld from someone through poverty, or through the state of civilisation into which he is born; but for the attainment of knowledge and skills in the higher worlds there is no obstacle for one who earnestly seeks for them.

Many believe that they must search here or there for the Masters of higher knowledge in order to receive enlightenment from them. But there are two possibilities. In the first place, whoever strives earnestly for higher knowledge will shun no exertion, fear no obstacle, in his quest for an Initiate who can lead him into the higher mysteries of the world. On the other hand, everyone may be certain that Initiation will come to find him under all circumstances, if he gives evidence of earnest and worthy endeavour to attain knowledge. It is a natural law among all Initiates to withhold from no man the knowledge he is entitled to possess; but there is equally a natural law which lays down that no occult knowledge shall be imparted to anyone not qualified to receive it. And the more strictly he observes both these laws, the more perfect is an Initiate. The spiritual bond embracing all Initiates is not an external one, but the two laws here mentioned form as it were strong clasps by which the members of this bond are held together. You may live in intimate friendship with an Initiate, yet a gap separates you from his essential self until you yourself have become an Initiate. You may win in the fullest sense the heart, the love, of an Initiate, but he will confide his secret to you only when you are ready for it. You may flatter him, you may torment him: nothing can induce him to divulge anything which he knows should not be divulged to you because at your present stage of development you do not understand how to prepare in your soul a worthy reception for this mystery.

The ways by which a man is made ready for the reception of a mystery are laid down with all exactitude. The direction he is to take is inscribed with indelible, eternal letters in the worlds of Spirit where the Initiates guard the higher mysteries. In ancient times, anterior to our 'history', the temples of the Spirit were outwardly visible; today, when our life has become so unspiritual, they are not to be found in the world open to external sight. But spiritually they are present everywhere, and everyone who seeks can find them.

Only within his own soul can a man find the means whereby the lips of the Initiates will be unsealed for him. He must develop certain faculties to a definite and high degree, and then the sublime treasures of the Spirit can become his own.

A certain fundamental attitude of the soul must be the starting-point. The spiritual investigator calls this fundamental attitude the *path of veneration*, of devotion to truth and knowledge. Without this fundamental attitude no one can become an occult pupil. Anyone who is experienced in this domain knows what aptitudes are shown already in their childhood by those who later on become occult pupils. There are children who look up with reverent awe to certain venerated persons. Their reverence for these people forbids them, even in the deepest depths of their hearts, to admit any thought of criticism or opposition. Such children grow up into young men and women who feel happy when they are able to look up to anything that fills them with veneration. Many occult pupils come from the ranks of such children. If you have ever stood outside the door of some revered person and on this your first visit had a feeling of awe as you pressed the door-handle to enter the room, which for you was a holy place, a feeling has come to expression within you which may be the seed of your later discipleship. It is a blessing for every maturing human being to have such feelings as foundations within him. But it must not be thought that this will lead to submissiveness and servility. What was once childlike veneration for persons becomes, later on, a veneration for truth and knowledge. Experience teaches that those of free bearing are those who have learnt to venerate where veneration is due; and veneration is due whenever it springs from the depths of the heart.

If we do not develop within ourselves the deeply rooted feeling that there is something higher than ourselves, we shall never find the strength to evolve to a higher stage. The Initiate has acquired the strength to lift his head to the heights of knowledge only by guiding his heart to the depths of veneration and devotion. The heights of the Spirit can be scaled only by passing through the gateway of humility. You can acquire true knowledge only when you have learnt to respect it. Man has certainly the right to turn his eyes to the light but he must first earn this right.

There are laws in the spiritual life just as there are in material life. Rub a glass rod with an appropriate substance and it becomes electrified, that is, it acquires the power to attract small objects. This is a law of Nature, known to everyone who has learnt a little physics. Similarly, acquaintance with the elementary rudiments of Spiritual Science brings the realisation that every feeling of *true* devotion harboured in the soul develops a power which leads sooner or later to a further stage of knowledge.

Whoever has within him feelings of true devotion, or who is fortunate enough to have them inculcated by a fitting education, brings a great deal with him when, later in life, he seeks access to higher knowledge. Failing such preparation, he will encounter difficulties at the very first step, unless he undertakes by rigorous self-education to engender within himself this attitude of devotion. In our time it is of the utmost importance that full attention be paid to this. Our civilisation tends more to criticism, judgment, condemnation, than to devotion and selfless veneration. Our children already criticise far more than they revere. But every criticism, every adverse judgment passed, dispels the powers of the soul for the attainment of higher knowledge, just as reverent veneration develops these powers. This is not meant to imply anything against our civilisation. There is no question here of levelling criticism against it. To this critical faculty, this conscious sense of human judgment, this principle of 'prove all things and hold fast what is best' we owe the greatness of our culture. Man could never have developed the science, industry, commerce, civil rights, of our time if he had not everywhere exercised his critical faculty and applied the standards of his judgment. But what we have thereby gained in the way of external culture, we have had to pay for with a corresponding forfeiture of higher knowledge, of spiritual life. It must be emphasised that in the domain of higher knowledge it is *not* a matter of venerating persons, but of venerating knowledge and truth.

We must clearly recognise, of course, that for an individual wholly involved in the externalised civilisation of our day it is very difficult to attain knowledge of the higher worlds. He can do so only if he works energetically on himself. In times when the conditions of material life were simple, the attainment of spiritual knowledge was easier. Whatever was worthy of veneration and reverence stood out in stronger relief from the things of the everyday world. In an epoch where criticism is universal, ideals are lowered. Other feelings take the place of veneration, reverence, worship and wonder. Our age thrusts these feelings more and more into the background, so that in everyday life they play a very small part. Whoever seeks higher knowledge must bring them to life in himself. He must himself instil them into his soul. This cannot be done through study; it can be done only through living. Whoever wishes to become a pupil of higher knowledge must therefore assiduously cultivate this attitude of devotion. Everywhere in his environment and in his experience he must look for whatever can capture his admiration and respect. If I encounter a human being and blame him for his weaknesses, I rob myself of the power of higher knowledge; but if I try to enter lovingly into his qualities, I muster this power. The pupil must bear this advice constantly in mind. Experienced spiritual investigators know how much power they owe to the circumstance that ever and again they look for the good in all things and withold critical judgment. But this must not remain an external rule of life; it must lay hold of our inmost soul. Man has it in his power to perfect himself and as time goes on completely to transform himself. But this transformation must take place in his inmost self, in his life of thought. It is not enough that I show respect to a person in my outward bearing; I must have this respect in my thoughts. The pupil must begin by bringing this devotion into his life of thought. He must be wary of thoughts of disrespect, of adverse criticism, and must endeavour straightway to cultivate thoughts of reverence.

Every moment that we set ourselves to discover whatever remains in our consciousness in the way of adverse, critical judgments of the world and of life—every such moment brings us nearer to higher knowledge. And we make rapid progress when in such moments we fill our consciousness with thoughts that imbue us with wonder, respect and veneration for the world and for life. Those experienced in these matters know that in every such moment powers are awakened which otherwise remain dormant. Thereby the spiritual eyes of man are opened. He begins to see things around him which formerly he had been unable to see. He begins to realise that hitherto he has seen only a part of the world. A human being standing before him now wears a quite different aspect. Certainly, this rule of life will not enable him to see what is described as the human aura. A still higher training is necessary for that. But he can fit himself for this higher training if he has previously undergone an unflagging training in devotional reverence.*

The treading of the path of knowledge by the pupil takes place silently, unnoticed by the outer world. No change need be noticed in him. He performs his duties and attends to his business as before. The transformation proceeds entirely in the inner recesses of the soul, hidden from outer sight. At first the pupil's whole inner life is irradiated by this basic mood of reverence for everything that is truly venerable. His whole life of soul finds its centre in this one basic feeling. Just as the sun's rays vivify everything living, so does reverence in the pupil vivify all sentient experiences of the soul.

It is not easy at first to believe that feelings such as those of reverence, respect and so on, have anything to do with cognition. This is because we are inclined to regard cognition as a faculty by itself, unrelated to other happenings

* In the last chapter of the book, *Theosophy: an Introduction to supersensible Knowledge of the World and the Destination of Man* (p. 146 of the 1965 edition), a survey of the 'Path of Knowledge' is given. The intention here is to indicate certain practical details.

in the soul. We forget that it is the *soul* which exercises the faculty of cognition; and feelings are for the soul what foodstuffs are for the body. If the body is given stones instead of bread, its activity will die away. So, too, with the soul. Veneration, respect, devotion, are nourishing foodstuffs which make the soul healthy and vigorous, especially in the activity of cognition. Disrespect, antipathy, under-estimation of what deserves recognition, exert a paralysing, withering effect on the faculty of cognition. For the spiritual investigator this fact is visible in the aura. A soul that cultivates feelings of reverence and devotion brings about a change in its aura. Certain spiritual colourings, as they may be called, yellowish-red, brownish-red in tone, give way to bluish-red tints. Thereby the faculty of cognition opens; it receives knowledge of facts in its environment of which previously it had no inkling. Reverence awakens a power of sympathy in the soul through which we draw towards us qualities in the beings around us, qualities which would otherwise remain concealed.

What can be achieved through devotion becomes still more effective when another trend of feeling is added. The individual learns to give himself up less and less to impressions of the outer world and to develop instead an active inner life. A person who darts from one impression of the outer world to another, who is all the time looking for distraction, does not find the way to occult science. The pupil must not blunt himself to the outer world, but be guided by his rich inner life in yielding himself to its impressions. When travelling through a beautiful mountain landscape, a man with depth of soul and wealth of feeling has experiences different from those of someone who is inwardly apathetic. Only what we experience within ourselves gives us the key to the beauties of the outer world. One person will sail across the sea and little in the way of experience passes through his soul; another hears the eternal language of the Cosmic Spirit; mysterious riddles of creation disclose themselves to him. We must learn how to make the best use of our own feelings and ideas if we want to develop a fruitful relationship with the outer world. In all its phenomena the outer world is filled with divine splendour, but we must first have experienced the Divine within ourselves if we are to discover it in the surrounding world.

The pupil is advised to arrange moments in his daily life for withdrawing into himself, in stillness and alone. But during these moments he should not occupy himself with the affairs of his own Ego: that would bring about the opposite of the aim in view. He should far rather allow what he has experienced and what the outer world has said to him to echo in the stillness. Every flower, every animal, every action, will then unveil to him secrets undreamed of. And thus he will prepare himself to see the outer world with quite different eyes. Anyone who is bent simply on enjoying one impression after another blunts his faculty of cognition; but if the enjoyment, once experienced, is allowed to *reveal* something, his cognition will be nurtured and trained. He must, however, accustom himself not merely to let the enjoyment echo on, but rather to renounce further enjoyment and work with inner energy upon the past experience. A dangerous pitfall lies in wait for him here. Instead of working inwardly, it is very easy to fall into the opposite habit of continuing to exploit the enjoyment even when it is over. Incalculable sources of error open up here: let no-one treat them lightly, The pupil must make his way through a host of tempters of his soul. They are all intent upon hardening his Ego and imprisoning it within itself; but he should open it widely to the world. He must indeed seek enjoyment, for only through enjoyment can the outer world approach him. If he blunts himself to enjoyment, he comes to be like a plant which can draw no nourishment from its environment. But if he stops short at the enjoyment he shuts himself up within himself. He will mean something only to himself, nothing to the world. However intensely he may live within himself, however vigorously he may cultivate his Ego—the world will reject him. For the world he is dead. The pupil regards enjoyment only as a means of ennobling himself for the world. Enjoyment is for him an emissary instructing him about the world; but after being instructed by enjoyment he goes forward to work. He does not learn in order to accumulate learning as his own treasure of knowledge, but in order to place this learning in the service of the world.

In all occult science there is a fundamental principle which cannot be transgressed if any goal is to be reached, and all occult training must instil it into the pupil. *All the knowledge you pursue merely for the enrichment of your own learning and to accumulate treasure of your own leads you away from your path; but all knowledge you pursue in order to grow more mature on the path of human ennoblement and world-progress brings you a step forward.*

This law must be inexorably observed, and no-one is an authentic pupil of higher knowledge until he has made it the guide-line of his whole life. This truth of spiritual training can be summed up in a short sentence: *Every idea that does not become your ideal kills a power in your soul; every idea that becomes an ideal engenders life-forces within you.*

Inner Tranquillity

The pupil is, to begin with, directed to the path of reverence and the development of the inner life. Spiritual Science also gives practical rules by which the path may be trodden and the inner life developed. These practical rules have no arbitrary origin. They are based upon ancient experiences and ancient wisdom and are given wheresoever the ways to higher knowledge are indicated. All true teachers of the spiritual life are in agreement as to the essential content of these rules, although they do not always clothe them in the same words. Minor differences, which are really only apparent, are due to matters which need not be discussed here.

No teacher of the spiritual life wishes to dominate other persons by means of such rules. He will not tamper with anyone's independence. Indeed, no one cherishes and protects a man's independence more zealously than the spiritual investigator. It was stated in the first section of this book that the bond of union embracing all Initiates is a spiritual one, and that two natural laws form clasps by which the members of this bond are held together. But if the Initiate leaves his enclosed spiritual domain and comes into public view, a third law must immediately be taken into account. —Adapt each single one of your actions and each single one of your words in such a way that you infringe upon no man's free will.

Anyone who has recognised that a true teacher of the spiritual life is permeated through and through by this attitude of soul can also be convinced that he forfeits no iota of his independence when he obeys the practical rules he is advised to follow.

One of the first of these rules can be expressed in words approximately as follows: 'Provide for yourself moments of inner tranquillity, and learn in these moments to distinguish the essential from the non-essential.' It is said advisedly, 'expressed in words'. All rules and teachings of spiritual science were originally given in a language of symbolic signs. And those who wish to know the full significance and extent of these teachings must first learn to understand this symbolic language. This understanding depends on the individual concerned having already taken the first steps in occult science. But he can take these steps if he has strictly observed such rules as are given here. The path is open to everyone whose will is sincere.

The rule concerning moments of inner tranquillity is simple; the observance of it is equally simple. But it leads to the goal only when the observance is as earnest and strict as it is simple in itself.

The pupil must set aside a short period of his daily life during which to concern himself with something altogether different from the objects of his daily occupation. And the way in which he occupies himself during this time must differ entirely from the activities which take up the rest of his day. But this must not be understood to mean that what he does in the time thus set apart has nothing to do with his daily work. On the contrary, he will soon notice that it is just these moments of seclusion, when used in the right way, which imbue him with strength to perform his daily tasks. Nor must it be supposed that the observance of this rule will deprive anyone of time essential for the fulfilment of his duties. If anyone were really to have no more time at his disposal, five minutes a day would suffice. What matters is how these five minutes are spent.

During these periods the individual should wrest himself

entirely free from his work-a-day life. His thoughts and life of feeling should assume a different colouring. He should let his joys, his sorrows, his cares, his experiences, his deeds, pass in review before his soul; and his attitude should be such that he looks at everything else in his experience from a higher standpoint.

We need only bear in mind how, in ordinary life, the view we take of the experiences and actions of another person differs altogether from the view we take of our own. This cannot be otherwise, for we are interwoven with our own experiences and actions; whereas we merely *observe* those of others. Our aim in these moments of seclusion must be to contemplate and judge our experiences and actions as though they were those of others, not our own. Suppose someone has suffered a hard blow of fate. How different his attitude would be towards a similar fate suffered by a fellow-being. Nobody can consider this attitude unjustifiable; it is inherent in human nature and applies equally to exceptional circumstances and to the everyday affairs of life. The pupil must at certain times look for the strength to stand towards himself as a stranger. He must confront his own self with the inner calmness of a judge. When this is accomplished, our own experiences show themselves to us in a new light. As long as we are entangled with them and stand, as it were, within them, we are connected as closely with the non-essential as with the essential. During a calm inner survey the essential separates from the non-essential. Sorrow and joy, every thought, every resolve, wear a different guise when we confront ourselves in this way. It is as though we had spent the whole day in some place where we saw the smallest and largest objects at the same close range, and in the evening climbed a neighbouring hill and surveyed the whole area at once. Then the proportions between the parts of the area will at once appear different from what they were when we were in the midst of them. This exercise will not and need not succeed with current dispensations of fate, but the pupil must attempt it in connection with those undergone in the past. The value of this inner, tranquil self-contemplation depends far less on *what* is actually contemplated than on finding within ourselves the strength which such inner tranquillity develops in us.

For every human being bears within himself a higher man, besides the everyday man, as we may call him. This higher man remains hidden until he is awakened, and he can be awakened only by each individual *himself*. But as long as this higher being is not awakened, the higher faculties which slumber in everyone and lead to supersensible knowledge will remain concealed.

As long as someone does not feel the fruits of inner tranquillity, he should say to himself that he must persevere with the earnest and strict observance of the rules indicated here. To one who thus perseveres the day will come when spiritual light will be all around him and a whole new world will be revealed to an inner eye of which he had previously been unaware.

Nothing need change in the outer life of the pupil because he is beginning to follow this new rule. He performs his duties as before; at first he endures the same suffering and experiences the same joy as before. In no way can he be estranged from life. Indeed, he can pursue his ordinary life more completely for the rest of the day because in the moments set apart he is acquiring a 'higher life'. Little by little this higher life will make its influence felt upon his everyday life. The tranquillity of the moments set apart will also have its effect upon his daily existence. In his whole being he will become more serene; he will acquire assurance and will no longer be disconcerted by incidental matters of every kind. Gradually he will become more and more his own guide, and will allow himself to be less and less led by circumstances and external influences. He will soon discover what a source of strength these periods of seclusion are for him. He will gradually cease to be angered by things that formerly angered him; countless things which formerly alarmed him will do so no longer. He acquires an entirely new outlook on life. Formerly he may have approached some task with anxiety, saying to himself: 'I lack the power to do this as well as I would wish.' Now this thought no longer comes to him, but a quite different one. Henceforth he says to himself: 'I will muster all my strength to do my work as well as I possibly can.' And he suppresses the thought that might make him anxious;

for he knows that anxiety might well impair his performance, and that in any case it cannot help him to do better. And thus thought after thought, fruitful and beneficial for his whole life, flow into the pupil's outlook. They take the place of thoughts which had a weakening, hampering effect upon him. He begins to steer his own ship on a steady course through the waves of life instead of leaving it to be driven hither and thither.

This calmness and certainty react upon the whole being. They bring about the growth of the inner man, and with the inner man those faculties which lead to higher knowledge. For it is by his progress in this direction that the pupil gradually reaches the point where he himself determines how the impressions of the outer world shall affect him. For example, he may hear a word spoken with the object of wounding or vexing him. Formerly he would indeed have been wounded or vexed, but now that he is treading the path to occult knowledge he is able to take from the word its wounding or vexing sting before it has found its way to his inner self. Or to take another example. A person easily becomes impatient when he is kept waiting. Then he begins to tread the path of knowledge. During his moments of inner tranquillity he permeates himself so fully with the feeling of the futility of impatience that henceforth, whenever he experiences impatience, this feeling is immediately present within him. The impatience that was about to assert itself vanishes, and an interval which would otherwise have been wasted through expressions of impatience will perhaps be filled by some worthwhile observation which can be made during the period of waiting.

Now the scope and significance of all this must be realised. Remember that the 'higher man' within man is in constant development. But it is only the tranquillity and certainty here described that make his orderly and regular development possible. The waves of external life press in upon the inner man from all sides if, instead of mastering this external life, he is mastered by it. Such a man is like a plant which has to grow in a rocky cleft. Its growth is stunted until new space is created for it. No external forces can create space for the inner man. Only the inner tranquillity he himself creates can do it. Outer conditions can alter the course of his outer life; they can never awaken the 'spiritual man' in him. It is the pupil—he alone—who must give birth to a new, higher man within himself.

This higher man then becomes the 'inner ruler' who directs the circumstances of the outer man with a sure hand. As long as the outer man is in control, the inner man is his slave and so cannot unfold his powers. If the fact of my getting angry or not depends upon something extraneous to myself, I am not master of myself, or—better said—I have not yet found the 'ruler within me'. I must develop the faculty of allowing the impressions of the outer world to approach me only in a way I myself determine; then only can I become a pupil in the real sense. And only in so far as the pupil earnestly seeks to develop this power can he reach the goal. It is not a matter of how far anyone can progress in a given time; the point is only that he should earnestly seek. Many have striven for years without noticing any appreciable progress; but many of those who did not despair, but remained unshaken, have then quite suddenly achieved the 'inner victory'.

In many walks of life great effort may well be needed to create these moments of inner tranquillity; but the greater the strength required, the more significant is the achievement. In occult science everything depends upon the pupil being able, with energy, inner truthfulness and uncompromising sincerity, to confront himself, and all his deeds and actions, as a complete stranger.

But only one side of the pupil's inner activity is characterised by this birth of his own higher being. Something else is needed also. Even when he confronts himself as a stranger it is only *himself* that he is contemplating; he is a spectator of those experiences and actions with which he is connected because of his particular situation in life. He must now disengage himself from this and rise above it to the purely *human* reality which no longer has anything to do with his particular circumstances. He must pass on to the contemplation of those things that would concern him as a man if he lived under quite different conditions and in a quite different situation. In this way something begins to live within him which transcends the personal. His gaze is directed to worlds higher than those with which everyday life connects him. And thus he begins to feel and realise as an actual experience that he belongs to these higher worlds. They are worlds concerning which his senses and his daily activities can say nothing. Thus he comes to move the central point of his being into his inner nature. He listens to the voices which speak to him in the moments of inner tranquillity; in his inner life he cultivates intercourse with the spiritual world. He is detached from the everyday world. Its hubbub is silenced; around him there is stillness. He rejects everything that reminds him of impressions from outside. Calm inner contemplation and converse with the purely spiritual world fill his whole soul. This calm contemplation must become a natural necessity for his life. To begin with he is completely absorbed in a world of thought, and he must develop a living feeling for this silent thought-activity. He must learn to love the inflow of the spirit that comes to him from it. He soon ceases to feel that this thought-world is less real than the everyday things around him. He begins to treat his thoughts as though he were dealing with external things, and then the moment approaches when he begins to feel that what reveals itself to him in the silence of inner thought-activity is much higher, much more real, than the things in space. He discovers that *life* expresses itself in this thought-world. He realises that thoughts are not mere shadow-pictures, but that hidden beings speak to him through them. Out of the silence something begins to speak to him. Formerly he heard it through his ear only;

now it resounds through his soul. An inner speech—an inner word—has revealed itself to him. When experienced for the first time, this moment is most blessed for the pupil. An inner light spreads out over his whole external world. A second life begins for him. The stream of a divine, bliss-bestowing world pours through him.

This life of the soul in thought, which widens more and more into a life in the spiritual reality of being, is called by the Gnosis and by Spiritual Science, *meditation* (contemplative reflection). Meditation of this order is the means by which supersensible knowledge is attained. But in such moments the pupil must not revel in feelings; he must not have vague, undefined sensations in his soul, for that would only hinder him from attaining true spiritual knowledge. His thoughts must be clear and sharply defined, and this aim will be furthered if he does not cling blindly to the thoughts that arise within him. Much rather should he steep himself in the lofty thoughts conceived in moments of meditation by men already advanced and inspired by the spirit. He should take as his starting-point writings which sprang from such revelation during meditation. In the literature of Mysticism, Gnosticism and modern Spiritual Science the pupil will find such writings, and therein material for his meditation. In these writings, seekers after the spirit have set down the thoughts of Divine Science which the Spirit has allowed to be proclaimed through its messengers to the world.

Through such meditation a complete transformation

takes place in the pupil. He begins to form entirely new conceptions of reality. All things acquire different values for him. It cannot be too often repeated that this transformation does not alienate him from the world. He will in no way be estranged from his daily round of duties, for he learns to realise that the most insignificant action he has to perform, the most insignificant experience that comes to him, are connected with cosmic beings and cosmic happenings. Once this connection becomes clear to him in his moments of contemplation, he sets about his daily activities with new and enhanced strength. For now he knows that he is working and suffering for the sake of a great cosmic and spiritual whole. Not indolence, but energy in life, springs from meditation.

With firm steps the pupil goes through life. No matter what it may bring him, he goes forward unbowed. In the past he did not know why he should work, why he should suffer, but now he knows. Obviously meditation leads more surely to the goal if carried out under the guidance of men of experience who know how everything may best be done. The advice and guidance of such men should be respected. No one will ever lose his freedom in these circumstances. Under this guidance, hesitant groping turns into work that is certain of its goal. Whoever applies to men with knowledge and experience in these matters will never ask in vain. But he must realise that he is seeking nothing more than the advice of a friend, not the domination of a would-be ruler. It will always be found that those with real knowledge are the most unpretentious of men, and that nothing is further from them than what people call the lust for power.

Whoever rises through meditation to the point where human nature is united with the spirit begins to kindle to life that which is eternal in him, that which is not confined within the boundaries of birth and death. The existence of this eternal reality can be doubted only by those who have not themselves experienced it. Thus meditation is the way which also leads man to knowledge and vision of the eternal, indestructible core of his being. And only through meditation can this vision come to man. Gnosis and Spiritual Science speak of the eternity of this core of being, of its reincarnation. The question is often asked: why do we know nothing of our experiences beyond the frontiers of birth and death? But the question should be put differently. The right question is: how is such knowledge acquired? In true meditation the path opens. Through meditation the remembrance of experiences beyond birth and death is revived. Everyone can acquire this knowledge; in all of us lie the faculties that can enable us to recognise and contemplate for ourselves what genuine Mysticism, Spiritual Science, Anthroposophy and Gnosis teach. But the right means must be chosen. Only a being with ears and eyes can be aware of sounds and colours; nor can the eye perceive if the light which makes things visible is wanting. Occult science offers the means whereby the spiritual ears and eyes are developed and the spiritual light is kindled.

The method of spiritual training may be described as consisting of three stages: (1) *Preparation:* this develops the spiritual senses. (2) *Enlightenment:* this kindles the spiritual light. (3) *Initiation:* this establishes intercourse with the higher Beings of the spiritual world.

THE STAGES OF INITIATION

The following communications form part of a spiritual training, the name and essential character of which will be understood by everyone who turns it to good account. They are connected with the three stages which in the school of spiritual life lead to a certain grade of Initiation. But only such teachings as may be imparted publicly will be found in this book. These indications are drawn from a much deeper and more intimate teaching. In occult training itself a quite definite course of instruction is followed. Certain practices help the soul of man to establish conscious intercourse with the spiritual world. These practices bear about the same relation to what will be communicated in the following pages as the instruction given in a higher, strictly disciplined school bears to the incidental teaching received in a preparatory school. Yet the earnest, persevering pursuit of what is indicated here can lead to genuine occult training. Impatient dabbling, devoid of earnestness and perseverence, can lead nowhere. The study of occult science can be successful only if the principles already set forth are strictly observed and progress is made on this basis.

The three stages indicated by the tradition mentioned above are as follows: (1) Preparation; (2) Enlightenment; (3) Initiation. It is not necessary for the first to be completed before the second is begun, or the second completed before the third is begun. In certain respects it is possible to partake of Enlightenment, even of Initiation, although in other respects one is still at the stage of Preparation. But it will be necessary to spend a certain time at the stage of Preparation before Enlightenment can begin. In the case of certain matters, at least, there must be Enlightenment before the stage of Initiation can begin. But for clarity's sake the three stages have to be described in sequence.

Preparation

Preparation consists of a very definite cultivation of the life of feeling and of thought, through which the 'body' of soul and spirit is equipped with higher instruments of sense and organs of activity, in the same way that forces of nature have equipped the physical body with organs moulded out of indeterminate living matter.

The first step is made by directing the attention of the soul to certain happenings in the world around us. Such happenings are, on the one hand, life that is budding, growing, thriving, and, on the other, all phenomena of fading, decay, withering. A man can see all this going on together whenever he turns his eyes, and in the nature of things it evokes feelings and thoughts in him. But in ordinary circumstances he pays too little attention to these thoughts and feelings. He hurries too quickly from one impression to another. The essential point is that he should fix his attention intently and consciously upon them. Wherever he observes a quite definite blossoming and thriving, he should banish everything else from his soul and for a short time give himself up entirely to this one impression. He will soon convince himself that a feeling which would previously have merely flitted through his soul now acquires a strong and energetic form. He must then allow this feeling to reverberate quietly within himself, while maintaining perfect inner calm. He must shut himself off from the rest of the outer world and follow only what his soul has to say about the phenomena of blossoming and thriving.

Yet it must not be thought that much progress can be made if the senses are blunted. First look at things in the world as keenly and precisely as you possibly can. Only then give yourself up to the feeling and the thought arising in the soul. What is important is that the attention should be directed with perfect inner equilibrium upon both activities. If you achieve the necessary tranquillity and if you surrender yourself to what arises in the soul, then, after a time, the following will be experienced.—Thoughts and feelings of a new character, unknown before, will be noticed rising up in the soul. Indeed, the more often the attention is turned alternately in this way upon something that is growing, blossoming and thriving, and then upon something that is fading and dying, the more animated will these feelings become. And just as natural forces build the eyes and ears of the physical body out of living substance, so will the organs of clairvoyance be built out of the feelings and thoughts thus evoked. A quite definite form of feeling is connected with growth and development; another, equally definite, with what is fading and dying. But this will come about only if an effort is made to cultivate these feelings in the way indicated.

It is possible to describe approximately what these feelings are like. A clear mental picture of them is within the reach of everyone who has these inner experiences. Anyone who has often turned his attention to the process of growing, blossoming and thriving will feel something remotely similar to the experience of a sunrise. And the process of fading and dying will evoke an experience comparable in the same way to the slow rising of the moon over the horizon. These feelings are two forces which, when properly nurtured and developed to an ever-increasing pitch, lead to the most significant results. A new world opens for anyone who systematically and deliberately surrenders himself again and again to such feelings. The soul-world, the so-called astral plane, begins to dawn before him. Growth and decay no longer remain facts which make vague impressions upon him. They form themselves into spiritual lines and figures of which he had previously known nothing. And these lines and figures differ according to the phenomena they represent. A blossoming flower, a growing animal or a dying tree will each conjure up a very definite form before his soul. The soul-world (the astral plane) slowly broadens out before him. These lines and figures have nothing arbitrary about them. Two pupils who have reached the appropriate stage of development will always see the same lines and figures in connection with the same phenomena. Just as a round table will be seen as round by two persons with normal sight and not as round by one and square by the other, so at the sight of a blossom, the same spiritual figure will present itself to two souls. And just as the forms of plants and animals are described in ordinary natural history, so does anyone versed in occult science describe the spiritual forms of the processes of growth and decay according to species and genus.

If the pupil has progressed so far that he can perceive the spiritual forms of phenomena which are also physically visible to his outer sight, he will then not be far from the stage of seeing things which have no physical existence and must therefore remain entirely hidden (occult) for anyone who has not received instruction in occult science.

It should be emphasised that the occult investigator must not lose himself in speculation as to the meaning of one thing or another. By such intellectualising he merely diverts himself from the right path. He should look out on the world with fresh, healthy senses and a keen power of observation, and then give himself up to his feelings. He should not try through intellectual speculation to determine what the things mean, but should rather allow the things themselves to tell him.*

A further important matter is *orientation*—as occult science calls it—in the higher worlds. This is achieved when the individual is permeated through and through with a conscious realisation that feelings and thoughts are *veritable realities*, just as are chairs and tables in the physical world of the senses. In the soul-world and in the world of thoughts, feelings and thoughts work upon each other just as physical objects do in the physical world. As long as anyone is not vividly imbued with this awareness he will not believe that a wrong thought he harbours may have as devastating an effect upon other thoughts in the realm of thoughts as the effect of a random bullet on the physical objects it hits. Such an individual may perhaps never allow himself to perform a physically visible act which he regards as senseless; but he will not shrink from harbouring wrong thoughts or feelings, because these appear to him to be harmless for the rest of the world. In occult science, however, progress is possible only when as much care is given to thoughts and feelings as to steps taken in the physical world. If someone sees a wall before him, he does not attempt to dash through it; he turns aside. In

* It should be remarked that *artistic* feeling, coupled with a quiet, introspective nature, is the best preliminary condition for the development of spiritual faculties. Artistic feeling pierces through the surface of things, and by so doing reaches their secrets.

other words, he conforms with the laws of the physical world.

There are such laws, too, for the world of feeling and thought, only they cannot impose themselves on man from without. They must flow out of the life of his own soul. This is achieved if he forbids himself at all times to harbour wrong thoughts and feelings. All arbitrary flitting hither-and-thither in thought, all capricious play of fancy, all fortuitous ebb and flow of emotion, must be forbidden. By observing this rule, nobody becomes poverty-stricken in feeling. On the contrary, if the inner life is regulated in this way the person will soon find himself becoming rich in feeling and in genuine imagination. Petty emotionalism and frivolous flights of thought are replaced by significant emotions and fruitful thoughts. Such feelings and thoughts lead man to orientate himself in the spiritual world. He establishes the right relationship to the things of that world, and this has a definite effect. Just as he, as physical man, finds his way between physical things, so now his path leads him between the phenomena of growing and withering which he has already come to know in the way described above. Then he follows all processes of growing and dying in a way that promotes his own advancement and the world's.

The pupil must also give further care to cultivating the world of *sound*. He must discriminate between the sounds produced by anything called *lifeless* (for example, a falling mass, a bell or a musical instrument) and sounds that come from a living creature (an animal or a human being). Someone who hears the sound of a bell may associate a feeling of pleasure with it; someone who hears the cry of an animal will discern in the sound, besides his own feeling, the expression of an inner experience of the animal, whether of pleasure or of pain. It is with this latter category of sounds that the pupil must set to work. He must concentrate his whole attention on the fact that the sound tells him of something that is foreign to his own soul, and he must sink himself into this foreign element. He must unite his own feeling inwardly with the pain or pleasure of which the sound tells him. He must be beyond caring whether *for him* the sound is pleasant or unpleasant, agreeable or disagreeable; his soul must be imbued only with what is going on in the being from whom the sound proceeds. Anyone who carries out such exercises with method and deliberation will acquire the faculty of mingling, as it were, with the being from whom the sound proceeds. To cultivate his life of feeling in this way will be easier for a person sensitive to music than for one who is unmusical. But let no one believe that a sense for music can be a substitute for this cultivation. The pupil of occult science must learn to respond in this way to the whole of nature. And by this means a new faculty will take root in the world of feeling and thought. Through her resounding tones, the whole of nature begins to whisper her secrets to the pupil. What he has previously experienced as incomprehensible noise will become an expressive language of nature herself. And whereas he had previously heard only sounds from the so-called lifeless world, he is now aware of a new language of the soul. If he makes further progress in this cultivation of his feelings, he will realise that he can hear things of which he knew nothing hitherto. He begins to *hear with the soul*.

Something more has still to be added in order that the highest point attainable in this particular field of experience may be reached. Of very special importance for the pupil's development is the way in which he *listens* to others when they are speaking. He must accustom himself to do this in such a way that, while listening, his own inner self is absolutely silent. When someone expresses an opinion and another listens, agreement or contradiction will generally be set astir in the listener. Many people will also feel impelled to voice their agreement, or more especially their disagreement. The pupil must silence all such inner agreement or disagreement. It is not a matter of suddenly altering his mode of life in such a way that he is striving to bring about this inner silence all the time. He will have to begin by doing so in particular cases, deliberately chosen. Then, quite slowly and by degrees, as of itself, this entirely new kind of listening will make its way into his habits.

In spiritual investigation this is systematically practised. The pupils are enjoined to listen at certain times, by way of practice, to the most contradictory views and to silence in themselves all positive agreement and, more especially all adverse criticism. The point is to silence not only all intellectual judgment, but also all feelings of displeasure, denial or agreement. The pupil must always watch himself carefully to see whether such feelings, even when not on the surface, may not still be present in the inmost core of his soul. He must listen, for example, to the utterances of those who in one respect or another are far beneath him, while yet suppressing every feeling of superiority or of possessing greater knowledge. It is useful for everyone to listen in this way to children, for even the wisest can learn immeasurably much from children. So the pupil comes to listen to the words of others quite selflessly, while completely shutting out his own personality, with its opinions and trends of feeling. When he has trained himself to listen without criticism, when even the most preposterous statement is made in his presence, he learns gradually to merge himself into the being of another. Then he hears *through* the words into the very soul of the other. It is through assiduous practice of this kind that sound becomes for the first time the right means for perceiving the soul and spirit. Certainly, this requires the most rigorous self-discipline, but it leads to a lofty goal. When these exercises are practised in connection with the others that have been indicated concerning the sounds of the world of nature, a new sense of hearing develops in the soul. The soul is now able to become aware of communications from the spiritual world which are not expressed in sounds perceptible to the physical ear. Perception of the 'inner word' awakens. Truths from the spiritual world gradually reveal themselves to the pupil. He hears himself addressed in a spiritual way.*

All higher truths are attained through such 'perception of the inner word'; and what we hear from the lips of a genuine spiritual investigator has been experienced by him in this way. But this does not mean that it is unnecessary to acquaint oneself with the literature of occult science before being able to hear this 'inner word' oneself. On the contrary, the reading of this literature and listening to the teachings given by occult science are themselves means of attaining personal knowledge. Every sentence of occult science is able to direct the mind to the point that must be reached if the soul is to make true progress. To all that has here been said must be added the zealous study of what the occult investigators communicate to the world. In all occult training such study belongs to the stage of Preparation. And anyone who might try all kinds of other methods would reach no goal if he did not absorb the teachings resulting from occult investigation. For because these teachings are drawn from the living 'inner word', from living perception of the 'inner word', they themselves have

* It is only to one who through selfless listening can become inwardly receptive in the real sense, in quietude and unmoved by any personal opinion or feeling, that the higher Beings of whom occult science tells, can speak. So long as a person directs any opinion any feeling, against what is to be heard, the Beings of the spiritual would keep silence.

spiritual life. They are not merely words: they are living powers. And while you follow the words of one versed in occult science, while you read a book that originates from genuine inner experience, powers are at work in your soul which make you clairvoyant, just as the forces of nature have created out of living substance your eyes and ears.

Enlightenment

Enlightenment is the result of very simple processes. Here, too, it is a matter of developing certain feelings and thoughts which slumber in every human being and must be wakened. Only one who with infinite patience carries through the simple processes strictly and with perseverance can be led to perception of the manifestations of the inner light. The beginning is made by studying different beings of nature in a particular way; for example, a transparent, beautifully formed stone (a crystal), a plant and an animal. One should endeavour, at first, to direct one's whole attention to a comparison of the stone with the animal. The thoughts here indicated as examples must pass through the soul accompanied by alert feelings, and no other thought, no other feeling, must intrude and disturb the intensely attentive contemplation. The pupil says to himself: 'The stone has a form; the animal too has a form. The stone remains motionless in its place; the animal changes its place. It is natural impulse (desire) which causes the animal to change its place. Natural impulses are more-over served by the animal's form. Its organs and limbs are in keeping with these impulses. The structure of the stone is not fashioned according to desires but by power that is void of desire'.*

If one thinks deeply into such thoughts, while contem-plating the stone and the animal with fixed attention, two quite different kinds of feelings will arise in the soul: one kind from the stone and the other from the animal. At first the attempt will probably not succeed, but little by little, by dint of genuine and patient practice, these feelings will ensue. This must be practised over and over again. At first the feelings are present only as long as the contem-plation lasts; later on their after-effects continue. And then they become something that remains alive in the soul. The student has then only to reflect and both feelings will always arise, even without contemplation of an external object. Out of these feelings and the thoughts connected with them, *organs of clairvoyance* are formed. If the plant is then included in the contemplation, it will be observed that the feeling emanating from it lies midway, both in character and degree, between the feeling that streams

* In its bearing on the contemplation of crystals, the facts here mentioned are in many ways distorted by those who have heard of them merely in an outer (exoteric) way, and this has led to practices such as crystal-gazing and the like. These practices are due to misunderstanding. They have been described in many books, but they never form the subject of genuine (esoteric) occult instruction.

from the stone and the feeling that streams from the animal.

The organs thus formed are eyes of the spirit. With them the pupil gradually learns to see something like psychic and spiritual colours. The spiritual world, with its lines and figures, remains dark as long as he has achieved only what has been described as Preparation; through Enlightenment it becomes light. Here, too, it must be noted that the words 'dark' and 'light' as well as the other expressions used, describe only approximately what is meant. Nothing more is possible if ordinary language is used, for this language was created for physical conditions only. When a stone is clairvoyantly observed, a colour streams from it which occult science describes as 'blue' or 'bluish-red'; and the emanation from an animal is described as 'red' or 'reddish yellow'. In reality, the colours seen are of a spiritual kind. The colour emanating from the plant is 'green', passing over into a light, ethereal rose-pink. The plant is a being which in higher worlds resembles, in a certain respect, its make-up in the physical world. This does not apply to the stone or the animal. It must be clearly understood that the above-named colours indicate only the main hues in the stone, plant and animal kingdoms. In reality there are intermediate nuances of every kind. Every stone, every plant, every animal, has its own quite definite nuance of colour. There are also the beings of the higher worlds who never incarnate physically; their colours are often wonderful, also often horrible. Indeed, the wealth of colour in these higher worlds is immeasurably greater than in the physical world.

Once a person has acquired the faculty of seeing with spiritual eyes, he encounters, sooner or later, the beings mentioned above, some of them higher than man in rank and some lower; they are beings who never enter physical existence.

If a man has reached the point described here, the ways to a great deal are open to him. But nobody should be advised to proceed still further without paying careful heed to what is said or otherwise communicated by the spiritual investigator. And with regard also to what has already been described, it is always best to pay attention to such experienced guidance. Moreover, if a man has the strength and endurance to reach the point denoting the elementary stages of Enlightenment, he will quite certainly seek and find the right guidance.

Under all circumstances, however, one precautionary measure is necessary, and whoever is unwilling to adopt it would be well advised to abstain from any attempt to make headway in occult science. It is essential that anyone who becomes a pupil should lose none of his qualities as a good, high-minded man, or his sensitivity to physical reality. Throughout his training, indeed, he must continually enhance his moral strength, his inner purity and his powers of observation. To take one example only: during the elementary exercises for Enlightenment the pupil must take care to ensure that his compassion for the human and animal worlds and his response to the beauty of nature are constantly increasing. Failing this care, the exercises would continually blunt his feelings and sensitivity; his heart would become hardened and the senses blunted. And that would inevitably lead to dangerous results.

How Enlightenment proceeds when, in line with the meaning of the foregoing exercises, the pupil passes from the stone, the plant and the animal up to man, and how, after Enlightenment, the union of the soul with the spiritual world takes place under all circumstances and leads on to Initiation—of this the following chapters will speak, in so far as this can be done.

In our time the path to occult science is sought by many. It is sought in all sorts of ways, and many dangerous, objectionable practices are tried. It is for this reason that those who claim to know something of the truth in these matters should make it possible for others to learn something about esoteric training. Only as much as conforms with this possibility has been communicated here. It is essential that something of the truth should become known in order to prevent error from causing great harm. No harm can come to anyone who follows the path here described, provided he does not force things. But one thing must be heeded: nobody should spend more time and strength on these exercises than his position in life and his duties allow. Nobody should immediately change anything in the external conditions of his life as the result of taking this path. Without patience, no genuine results can be achieved. After a few minutes the pupil must be able to stop the exercises and quietly go about his daily tasks. No thoughts about the exercises should interfere with this. Whoever has not learnt to *wait* in the highest and best sense of the word will never achieve results of real value.

Control of Thoughts and Feelings

When anyone seeks the paths leading to higher knowledge in the way described in the preceding pages, he should not omit to fortify himself throughout his efforts with one continuous thought. He must constantly have in mind that after some time he may have made quite considerable progress without this being apparent to him in the way he may have expected. Whoever forgets this may easily lose perseverance and after a short time relinquish all attempts. The powers and faculties to be developed are, at the beginning, of a very delicate kind, and differ entirely from any ideas that may have been previously formed of them by the individual concerned. After all, he will have been accustomed to occupy himself with the physical world alone; things of the soul and spirit will have been far from his sight and mind. It is therefore not surprising that when these new powers of spirit and soul are developing within him, he should not be immediately aware of them. Here lies the possibility of error for anyone who sets out on the path to occult knowledge without guidance from the experiences gathered by competent investigators. The occultist is aware of the progress made by the pupil long before the latter is conscious of it. He knows how the delicate eyes of spirit are beginning to develop before the pupil has any notion of it. And a large part of what the occultist has to say will be designed to keep the pupil from losing confidence and endurance before the pupil gains knowledge of his own progress. The occultist, as we know, can give his pupil nothing that does not already lie hidden within him. All he can do is to give guidance for the development of slumbering faculties. But what he communicates from his own experiences will be a support for one who is striving to find his way out of darkness to the light.

Many abandon the path to occult science soon after having set foot upon it because their progress is not immediately apparent to them. And even when the first experiences begin to arise, the pupil often regards them as illusions because he had formed quite different ideas of what they were going to be. He loses courage, either because he considers these first experiences valueless or because they seem to him so insignificant that he does not believe they could lead him to any important results within a measurable time. Courage and self-confidence are two beacons which must never be extinguished on the path to occult science. No one will ever travel far who cannot bring himself to repeat, over and over again, an exercise which has failed, apparently, for an incalculable number of times.

Long before there is any distinct perception of progress, a dim feeling arises of being on the right path. This feeling should be cherished and fostered, for it can become a trustworthy guide. Above all it is imperative to eradicate the belief that any weird, mysterious practices are required for the attainment of higher knowledge. Let it be clearly realised that the starting-point must be the feelings and thoughts of man's everyday life and that these feelings and thoughts need only be given a new, unfamiliar direction. Everyone must say to himself: 'In my own world of feeling and thought the loftiest mysteries lie hidden, only I have hitherto not been aware of them.' In the end it all depends on the fact that man ordinarily carries body, soul and spirit about with him but is conscious in a true sense only of his body, not of his soul and spirit. The pupil of occult science becomes conscious of the soul and spirit just as ordinary man is conscious of his body. Hence the important thing is to give the thoughts and feelings the right direction, for only then can one develop perception of things that are invisible in everyday life. One of the ways by which this can be done will now be indicated. Again, like almost everything else so far considered, it is a simple matter, but its effects are of the greatest consequence if it is perseveringly carried through in a mood of sufficient sensitivity.

Let the pupil place before him a small seed of a plant.

The point is to intensify the right kind of thoughts while contemplating this insignificant object and through these thoughts to develop certain feelings. First, let him realise clearly what his eyes are actually seeing. Let him describe to himself the shape, colour, and all other distinctive features of the seed. Then let him reflect as follows: 'Out of this seed, if planted in the soil, there will grow a plant of complex structure.' Let him visualise this plant, build it up in his imagination and then say to himself: 'What I am now picturing in my imagination will later be drawn out of the seed by the forces of the earth and the light. If I had before me an artificial object which imitated the seed to such a deceptive degree that my eyes could not distinguish it from a real seed, no forces of the earth or light could call forth a plant from it.' Whoever lays hold of this thought quite clearly, so that it becomes an inner experience, will be able to unite the following thought with the right feeling. He will say to himself: 'All that will ultimately grow out of the seed is already secretly enfolded within it as the *force* of the whole plant. In the artificial imitation of the seed no such force is present. And yet to my eyes both appear alike. The real seed therefore contains something invisible, which is not present in the imitation.' It is to this invisible something that thought and feeling are now to be directed.* Let the pupil picture the

* Anyone who might object that a microscopical examination would reveal the difference between the real seed and the imitation would only show that he had failed to grasp the point. The

following to himself: This invisible something will presently transform itself into the visible plant which I shall have before me in shape and colour. Let him hold firmly to the thought: The invisible will become visible. If I could not think, then that which will become visible only later could not already announce its presence to me.

Particular emphasis must be laid on the following point: what is being thought here must also be intensely *felt*. In inner quiet the thought indicated above must be *experienced*, with no disturbing intrusions from other thoughts. And sufficient time must be allowed for the thought and feeling united with it to penetrate the soul. If this is brought about in the right way, then, after a time—possibly only after many attempts—an inner force will make itself felt. And this force will create a new power of perception. The grain of seed will appear as if enveloped in a small, luminous cloud. In a sensory-spiritual way it will be felt as a kind of flame. The centre of this flame evokes the same impression as that made by the colour lilac; the edges give the impression of a bluish tint. Something formerly not seen is here revealed, created by the power of the thoughts and feelings that have been inwardly stirred into activity. The plant itself, which will become physically visible only later on, now manifests in a spiritually visible way.

---

aim of the exercise is not to examine the object as seen by the physical senses, but to use it in order to develop forces of soul and spirit.

It is understandable that many people will regard all this as illusion. They will say: 'What is the use to me of such visions, such fantasies?' And many will abandon the path. But this is precisely the all-important point: not to confuse fantasy with spiritual reality at these difficult stages of development; and then to have the courage to press forward and not to become timorous and faint-hearted. On the other hand, however, it must be emphasised that the healthy reason which distinguishes truth from illusion must be continually cultivated. During all these exercises the individual must never lose his fully conscious self-control. He must practise the same reliable thinking that he applies to the details of everyday life. It would be very bad to lapse into day-dreams. Intellectual clarity, not to speak of sober commonsense, must at every moment be maintained. And it would be the greatest mistake if as the result of such exercises the pupil were to lose his mental balance; if he were drawn away from judging the affairs of his daily life as clearly and soundly as before. He should examine himself again and again to see if his mental equilibrium has been at all disturbed, and whether he has remained unaltered in relation to his daily circumstances.

He must preserve an unshakable inner serenity and a clear mind for everything. Strict care must always be taken not to give oneself up to arbitrary daydreams or to all sorts of different exercises. The directions indicated above have been tested and practised since time immemorial and no others are communicated here. Anyone attempting to turn to exercises of a different kind which he has himself devised, or of which he has heard or read somewhere or other, will inevitably go astray and find himself on the path of boundless fantasy.

A further exercise, to be linked on to the one just described, is the following. Let the pupil place before him a fully developed plant. Now let him fill his mind with the thought: The time will come when this plant will wither and die. Nothing of what I now see before me will then exist. But the plant will have developed seeds, and these in their turn will grow into new plants. Again I become aware that in what I see, something I do not see lies hidden. I fill my mind with the thought: This plant, with its form and colours, will in time be no more. But the fact that it produces seeds teaches me that it will not vanish into nothingness. At present I cannot see with my eyes what preserves it from disappearance, any more than I could previously see the plant in the seed. Hence there is something in the plant that my eyes do not see. If I let this thought live in me, imbued with the feeling that should go with it, then in due time there will again develop in my soul a force which will become new vision. Again there will grow out of the plant a kind of spiritual flame-form, correspondingly larger, of course, than the one previously described. It may give an impression of blue in the middle and of yellowish-red at the outer edge.

It must be explicitly emphasised that these 'colours' are not colours as seen by physical eyes. To apprehend 'blue' spiritually means to be aware of or to feel something similar to what is experienced when the physical eye rests on the colour blue. This must be borne in mind by anyone who is intent upon rising gradually to the level of spiritual perceptions. Otherwise he will expect to find in the spiritual a mere repetition of the physical, and that would lead to the most bitter bewilderment.

Whoever has achieved this spiritual sight has gained a great deal, for things reveal themselves not only in their present state of being but also in their stages of formation and passing away. Everywhere he begins to see the spirit, hidden from the physical eyes. And thus he has taken the first step towards penetrating with his own vision behind the mystery of birth and death. For the outer senses, a being comes into existence at birth and passes away at death. But that is only because these senses do not perceive the hidden spirit of the being. For the spirit, birth and death are merely transformations, just as the sprouting of the flower from the bud is a transformation enacted before our physical eyes. But if we wish to gain direct knowledge of this through our own vision we must first waken the necessary spiritual sense in the way indicated here.

In order to dispose immediately of another objection which might be raised by certain people who have some psychic experience, something more must be said. It is certainly not disputed that there are shorter and simpler paths, and that many people have come to know the phenomena of birth and death through their own vision without having first gone through all that has been described here. There are indeed people with considerable psychic gifts, needing only a slight stimulus to bring their gifts to fruition. But they are exceptions. The path described here is safer and more generally suitable. It is possible to acquire some knowledge of chemistry by exceptional methods, but if you wish to become a chemist you must follow the recognised and more reliable course.

It would be a serious mistake for anyone to suppose that he could reach the goal more convincingly if the grain of seed or the plant mentioned above were merely pictured, merely visualised in the imagination. This might also lead to the goal, but not as surely as the method indicated here. The vision attained in that way will, in most cases, be only a figment of the imagination, and the transformation of it into genuine spiritual vision will still have to be accomplished. For the point is not that I arbitrarily create visions for myself, but that reality creates them in me. The truth must well up from the depths of my own soul; but the magician who conjures forth the truth must not be my ordinary ego but the actual beings whose spiritual reality I want to behold.

If as a result of exercises of this kind the pupil has discovered in himself the rudimentary beginnings of spiritual perception, he may proceed to the contemplation of man himself. Simple phenomena of human life must be chosen to begin with. But before making any attempts in this direction it is imperative that he should work with particular earnestness at the thorough purification of his moral character. He must banish every thought of ever using for his own personal benefit knowledge gained in this way. He must be sure in his mind that he will never turn to evil account any power he may gain over his fellow-men. Hence everyone who is seeking to discover the mysteries of human nature through his own vision must obey the golden rule of genuine occult science. This golden rule is as follows: For every *one* step forward that you take in seeking knowledge of occult truths, take *three* steps forward in the improvement of your own character. If this rule is observed, such exercises as the following may be attempted.

Recall to mind someone whom you may have observed when he was filled with desire for some object. Attention should be focused on the desire itself. It is best to recall to memory the moment when the desire was keenest and it was still uncertain whether the object of the desire would or would not be attained. And now give yourself up entirely to the mental picture of the recollection. Maintain the utmost inner calm in your own soul. Make the greatest possible effort to be blind and deaf to everything else that is going on around you, and take special care that through the mental picture thus evoked a *feeling* is awakened in the soul. Let this feeling rise in your soul like a cloud on an empty horizon. As a rule, naturally, the contemplation will be interrupted because the person on whom your attention is fixed was not observed in the relevant state of soul for a sufficient length of time. There will probably be hundreds and hundreds of unavailing attempts. But patience must not be lost. After many attempts you will succeed in bringing things to the point of experiencing in your own soul a feeling corresponding to the state of soul of the individual observed. After a time you will notice that this feeling elicits in your soul a force that becomes a spiritual perception of the other's state of soul. A picture seeming to be luminous will appear in your field of vision. And this spiritually luminous picture is the so-called astral embodiment of the state of soul caused by the desire. Again the impression given by this picture may be described as flame-like, yellowish-red in the middle and reddish-blue or lilac at the edge. Much depends upon treating such a spiritual perception with delicacy. It is best not to speak to anyone about it, except to your teacher, if you have one. For if an attempt is made to describe such phenomena in clumsy words, this generally leads to subtle delusions. Words in everyday use are not meant for such matters and are therefore too gross and ponderous. The consequence is that through the attempt to clothe the experience in words one is misled into mixing all kinds of fanciful delusions with the actual perceptions. Here again is an important rule for the pupil: know how to be silent about your spiritual experiences. Be silent about them even to yourself. Do not attempt to clothe in words what you see in the spirit, or to puzzle over it with the clumsy intellect. Lend yourself freely to your spiritual perception and do not disturb yourself by pondering over it a great deal. For you must remember that at the beginning your power of reflection is by no means on a level with your vision. You have acquired this faculty of reflection in a life hitherto confined to the physical world of sense, and the faculty you are now acquiring transcends that world. Therefore do not try to apply to the new, higher faculty, the standard of the old. Only one who has already gained some certainty and steadiness in the observation of inner experiences can speak about them in such a way that his fellow-men will be stimulated by what he says.

The exercises just described may be supplemented by the following. Observe in the same way someone to whom the fulfilment of some wish, the gratification of some desire has been granted. If the same rules and precautions as indicated for the other case are followed, the attainment of spiritual perception will also be possible here. A spiritual flame-form will be observed, creating an impression of yellow in the middle, with greenish edges.

Through observing his fellow-men in this way the pupil may easily succumb to a moral defect. He may become unloving, uncharitable. Every conceivable effort must be made to ensure that this does not happen. Such observation should be practised only by one who has already risen to the level at which he is fully convinced that thoughts are realities. He must then no longer allow himself to think of his fellow-men in a way that is incompatible with the highest reverence for human dignity and human liberty.

The thought that a human being could be merely an object for observation must never for a moment be entertained. The aim of self-education must be to ensure that every occult observation of human nature goes hand in hand with unlimited respect for the rights of every individual and with a recognition—both in thoughts and in feelings—that what lives in each human being is sacred and inviolable. A feeling of reverence for everything human must fill us, even when it is only in retrospect.

For the present these two examples will be enough to show how enlightened insight into human nature is achieved; they can at least point out the path to be followed. The soul of anyone who has achieved the inner calm and tranquillity necessary for such observation will undergo a great transformation; and this will soon reach the point where the inner enrichment of his being gives confidence and composure to his outer behaviour. This in turn will react upon his soul and he will be able to help himself further along the path. He will find ways and means of discovering in human nature more and more that is hidden from the external senses; and he will then be ready also for insight into the mysterious connections between human nature and everything else in the universe.

By following this path the pupil comes nearer and nearer to the moment when he can take the first steps of *Initiation*, but before this can be done, one thing more is necessary. This necessity may at first be far from apparent to the pupil, but later on he will be convinced of it.

What the would-be Initiate must bring with him is a certain mature courage and fearlessness. He must go out of his way to find opportunities through which these qualities are developed. In occult training they should be cultivated systematically. But in this respect life itself is a good school—perhaps the best of all. The pupil must be prepared to look danger calmly in the face and be resolute to overcome difficulties unswervingly. For instance, when faced with some danger he must immediately bring himself to realise: my fear is utterly useless; I should have none of it, but rather think only of what is to be done. And he must reach the point where, in circumstances when he would formerly have been fearful, 'to be frightened', 'to lack courage', are out of the question for him, at least in his inmost self. By self-discipline in this direction a man develops in himself very definite forces which he needs if he is to be initiated into higher mysteries. Just as physical man needs nervous forces in order to use his physical senses, so as a being of soul he needs the force which is developed only in courageous, fearless natures. Whoever presses forward to the higher mysteries sees things which the illusions of the senses conceal from ordinary human beings. For if the physical senses do not allow him to behold the higher truth, they are for this very reason his benefactors. They hide from him things which, if he were unprepared, would throw him into utter disarray; the sight of them would be more than he could endure. The pupil must be able to endure this sight. He loses certain supports in the outer world which he owed to his entanglement in illusion. It is literally as if the attention of someone were called to a danger of which he has known nothing, although it has been hovering round him for a long time. Hitherto he had felt no fear, but now that he knows, fear overcomes him, although the danger has not been increased by his awareness of it.

In the world there are constructive and destructive forces: the destiny of manifested being is to come into existence and to pass away. The seer has to penetrate into the working of these forces and the course of destiny. The veil screening the eyes of spirit in everyday life must be removed. But man is himself interwoven with these forces, with this destiny. In his own nature there are destructive and upbuilding forces. To the eyes of the seer his own soul is revealed as undisguisedly as other objects are. The pupil must not lose strength in the face of this self-knowledge. And only if he brings a surplus with him will his strength not fail. To this end he must learn to maintain inner calm and steadiness in difficult circumstances of life; he must cultivate in himself a strong trust in the beneficent powers of existence. He must be prepared to find that many motives which had actuated him hitherto will do so no longer. He will have to realise that hitherto he has thought and done many things only because he was in the toils of ignorance. Such reasons as were formerly his will disappear. He did many things out of vanity; now he will see how utterly futile vanity is for the seer. He did many things out of the desire for possessions; now he will realise how destructive all desire for possessions is. He will have to develop quite new motives for thinking and acting and it is here that courage and fearlessness are required.

It is preeminently a question of cultivating this courage and this fearlessness in the inmost depths of the life of thought. The pupil must learn not to despair over failure. He must be capable of the thought: 'I will forget that I have once more failed in this matter and will try again as if nothing had happened.' In this way he struggles through to the conviction that the sources of strength in the universe upon which he can draw are inexhaustible. He struggles ever onwards to the spirit which will uplift and support him, however weak and feeble his earthly nature may have proved to be. He must be able to press on into the future, undismayed by any experiences of the past. If the pupil has acquired these faculties to a certain extent, he is then mature enough to learn the true *names* of things, and these names are the key to higher knowledge. For Initiation consists in learning to call the things of the world by the names they bear in the spirit of their divine Originators. In these names their mysteries lie. The Initiates speak a language different from that of those who are not initiated because they designate created things by the very names which created them.

The next chapter will speak of Initiation itself—in so far as this is possible.

INITIATION

Initiation is the highest stage of esoteric training concerning which indications that will be generally intelligible can be given in writing. Communications concerning all that lies beyond it are difficult to understand; but this further path can be found by everyone who through Preparation, Enlightenment and Initiation has pressed forward to the lower mysteries.

The knowledge and proficiency imparted to an individual by Initiation are an endowment he could not otherwise acquire until a far-distant future, after many incarnations, by quite different means and in a quite different form. Anyone who is initiated today experiences something that he would otherwise experience much later, under quite different conditions.

An individual can learn of the mysteries of existence only as much as corresponds with his degree of maturity. It is for this reason only that the path to the higher stages of knowledge and capacity is beset with obstacles. No one should use a firearm until he has had sufficient experience to avoid causing damage with it. If someone were initiated today without the necessary preliminaries, he would lack the experience still to be acquired through incarnations in the future, until the mysteries in question become known to him in the normal course of his development.

At the Portal of Initiation, therefore, these experiences must be replaced by something else. Hence the first instructions given to the candidate for Initiation provide a substitute for future experiences. These are the so-called 'Trials' he has to undergo; they are in fact a normal consequence of the life of soul when exercises such as those described in the preceding chapters are continued in the right way.

These Trials are often written about in books, but it is only natural that through such descriptions quite false ideas of their nature are evoked. For a person who has not passed through the stages of Preparation and Enlightenment will know nothing about these Trials and is therefore unable to describe them accurately.

Certain things and facts belonging to the higher worlds will inevitably come into contact with the would-be Initiate. But he will be able to see and hear them only if he has come to perceive spiritual forms of colours, tones and so on, described in the chapters on Preparation and Enlightenment.

The first 'Trial' consists in acquiring a truer vision than the average man possesses of the corporeal attributes of lifeless things, then of plants, animals and human beings. This does not mean what is called scientific knowledge today, for it is a question not of science but of vision. As a rule the process is that the would-be Initiate learns how the things of nature and living beings manifest themselves to the spiritual ear and the spiritual eye. In a certain way these beings and things then lie disclosed—naked—before the beholder. The qualities which are there heard and seen are concealed from the physical eye and the physical ear. They are hidden from sensory perception as though behind a veil. The falling away of this veil for the would-be Initiate is connected with a process known as 'spiritual burning away'. Hence this first Trial is called the 'Trial by Fire'.

For many human beings, everyday life is itself a more or less unconscious process of Initiation through the Trial by Fire. Such people have passed through manifold experiences of such a kind that their self-confidence, courage and fortitude have been enhanced in a healthy way, and they learn to bear sorrow, disappointment and failure in undertakings with greatness of soul, and above all with equanimity and unbroken strength. Whoever has undergone experiences of this kind is often an Initiate without definitely knowing it, and then only a little is needed to open his spiritual ears and eyes so that he becomes a seer. For it must be realised that in a genuine Trial by Fire it is not a matter of satisfying the curiosity of the candidate. True, he learns to know many remarkable facts of which others have no inkling. But this acquisition of knowledge is not the goal; it is only the means to the goal. The goal is that through knowledge of the higher worlds the candidate acquires greater and truer self-confidence, enhanced courage and a magnanimity and quality of endurance quite different from anything that can generally be acquired in the lower world.

After the Trial by Fire, every candidate may still turn back. Strengthened in both soul and body, he will then resume his life and wait for a future incarnation to continue the process of Initiation. In his present incarnation, however, he will be a more useful member of society than he was before. In whatever situation he may find himself, his steadiness, circumspection, beneficent influence over his fellow-men and his fixity of purpose will have increased.

If, after completing the Trial by Fire, the candidate wishes to continue the esoteric training, a certain script, generally adopted in such training, must be disclosed to him. The true esoteric teachings reveal themselves in this script because the really hidden (occult) content of things can neither be directly expressed in the words of ordinary language nor set forth in ordinary writing. Those who have learnt from the Initiates translate the teachings of occult science into ordinary language as best they can. The occult script reveals itself to the soul when the soul has developed spiritual perception, for it is inscribed enduringly in the spiritual world. It cannot be learnt as artificial writing is learnt and read. The candidate grows in the appropriate way towards clairvoyant knowledge and during this process there develops in him, as a faculty of soul, the power impelling him to 'decipher' the happenings and beings of the spiritual world as he would decipher the characters of a script. This power, and with it the experience of the corresponding 'Trial', might possibly waken in the soul as though of its own accord, with the soul's advancing development. But the goal will be reached with greater certainty by following the directives given by experienced investigators who are skilled in deciphering the occult script.

The signs of the occult script are not arbitrarily devised, but correspond to the forces actively working in the world. The language of things is learnt through these signs. It becomes immediately apparent to the candidate that the signs he is now coming to know correspond to the figures, colours, tones, and so on which he learnt to perceive during the stages of Preparation and Enlightenment. He realises that everything he had previously learnt was only like learning to spell. Now for the first time he is beginning to read in the higher world. The separate shapes, tones and colours are now revealed to him as forming a great, inter-connected whole. Now for the first time he has real certainty in observing the higher worlds. Previously he could never be positive whether the things he saw were seen correctly. And now, at last, a systematic understanding is possible between the candidate and the Initiate in the domain of higher knowledge. For whatever the association between an Initiate and another individual may be in everyday life, the higher knowledge in its direct form can be imparted by the Initiate only in the sign-language already described.

Through this language the pupil becomes acquainted also with certain rules of conduct, and with certain duties of which he had known nothing. Having come to know these rules he can perform actions endowed with a significance such as the actions of one who is not initiated can never possess. He acts from out of the higher worlds. Indications for such actions can be understood only in terms of the occult script.

But it must be emphasised that there are individuals who are unconsciously capable of performing such actions, although they have never undergone an esoteric training. Such 'helpers of the world and of humanity' lead lives of blessing and good deeds. For reasons not to be discussed here, they have been endowed with gifts which seem supernatural. What distinguishes them from the pupil of occult science is only that the latter acts with consciousness and with full insight into the whole situation. He acquires by training what has been bestowed on the others by higher Powers for the well-being of humanity. Those upon whom divine Grace has been bestowed can be truly revered; but the work of training should not for this reason be considered superfluous.

Once the student has learnt the sign-script, a further 'Trial' begins for him. This is to prove whether he can move with freedom and certainty in the higher worlds. In everyday life a man is impelled to action by inducements from outside. He works at some occupation because one duty or another is imposed upon him by circumstances. It need hardly be mentioned that the pupil must neglect none of his duties in everyday life *because* he is living in higher worlds. No duty in a higher world can force anyone to neglect a single one of his duties in the ordinary world. The father will remain just as good a father to his family, the mother just as good a mother; neither an official nor a soldier nor anyone else will be kept from any duties if they become pupils of occult science. On the contrary, all the qualities which make a human being efficient in life are enhanced in the pupil to a degree of which the uninitiated can form no idea. If to him this enhancement is often not apparent—though sometimes it may be—this is only because he is not always capable of judging the Initiate correctly. What the latter does is not always immediately intelligible to the former. But this, too, is noticeable only in special cases.

For one who has reached this stage of Initiation there are duties for which no stimulus comes from outside. He will then be moved to action not by external conditions, but only by the rules of conduct revealed to him in the hidden script. Through this second 'Trial' he must now show that, guided by such a rule, his actions have the same reliability and firmness as those of an official performing the duties that devolve upon him. To this end, the candidate will find himself faced in the course of his training with a definite task. He has to perform some action in consequence of observations made on the basis of what he has learnt during the stages of Preparation and Enlightenment. And he must recognise what he has to do through the understanding he has acquired of the occult script. If he recognises his duty and acts rightly, he has been successful in the

Trial. His success can be known from the alteration produced by his action in the patterns, colours and tones apprehended by his spiritual ears and eyes. As the training progresses, exact indications are given of what the patterns and so on look like after the action has been performed, and the candidate must know how and why he was able to bring about the change. This Trial is known as the 'Trial by Water' because in his activity in these higher realms the candidate lacks any support from outer circumstances, just as support is lacking when someone moves about in water that is out of his depth. The procedure must be repeated until the candidate has gained perfect assurance under these conditions.

This Trial, too, is concerned with acquiring a certain quality. Through his experiences in the higher worlds the candidate develops this quality in a short time to such a high degree that he could normally have acquired it only after many more incarnations. The essential thing is that in order to bring about in the higher realms of existence the change referred to, he must follow only what is based upon his higher perception and his reading of the occult script. Should he, in the course of his action, introduce any element of his own wishes, opinions, and so forth, or should he for one moment evade the laws he has recognised to be right in order to indulge his own arbitary will, the result would be altogether different from what should properly come about. In this case the candidate would at once lose sight of the goal of his action, and confusion would set in.

Throughout this Trial, therefore, the candidate has abundant opportunity to develop his self-control. And that is what matters above all. Here, again, those whose life before Initiation has led them to acquire self-control will find it easier to undergo this Trial successfully. Whoever has acquired the faculty of following high principles and ideals while setting aside personal predilections, whoever is capable of always performing his duty when inclinations and sympathies are only too ready to divert him from it— such a one is unconsciously an Initiate even in everyday life. And only a little will still be necessary to enable him to succeed in this Trial. Indeed, it must even be said that a certain degree of Initiation already unconsciously gained in life will be indispensable for success in this second Trial. For just as it is difficult for many people who have not learnt to write properly in their childhood to make good this deficiency when they have reached maturity, so too it is difficult to develop the necessary degree of self-control at the moment of insight into the higher worlds if a certain measure of it has not been acquired in everyday life. The things of the physical world do not alter, whatever our wishes, desires and inclinations may be. In the higher worlds, however, our wishes, desires and inclinations have an actual effect on things. If we want to produce a particular effect in these worlds we must have ourselves completely under control; we must follow the right principles only and be subject to no arbitrary impulse.

A human quality that comes into very special consideration at this stage of Initiation is an absolutely healthy and
reliable faculty of judgment. Attention should be paid to
the training of this faculty during all the earlier stages; and
this will show whether the candidate is equipped for the
true path of knowledge. Further progress is possible only if
he can distinguish illusion, meaningless pictures of fancy,
superstitions and phantasmagoria of every kind, from
reality. This is at first more difficult at the higher stages
of existence than at the lower. Every preconception, every
cherished opinion with regard to the things in question,
must disappear; truth alone must guide. There must be
perfect readiness to abandon any idea, opinion or inclination directly logical thought demands it. Certainty in
higher worlds is to be attained only when one's personal
opinion is never cherished.

Individuals whose mode of thinking tends to fanciful-
ness and superstition can make no progress on the path to
occult knowledge. It is a precious treasure that the pupil
is to acquire. All doubt about the higher worlds passes from
him. With all their laws they reveal themselves to him.
But he cannot have this good fortune as long as he allows
himself to be the prey of phantasmagoria and illusions.
It would go badly for him if his imagination and his preconceptions were to run away with his intellect. Dreamers
and fancy-ridden individuals are as unfit for the path to
occult knowledge as those who are under the sway of
superstitions. This cannot be over-emphasised, for the

most sinister enemies on the path to knowledge in the higher worlds lurk in phantasies, day-dreams and superstitions. Yet nobody need believe that the pupil loses all sense of the poetry in life, all power of enthusiasm, because the words: 'All prejudice must leave you,' are written over the portal leading to the second Trial, or because at the portal leading to the first Trial, he must read: 'Without healthy human reason, all your steps are taken in vain.'

If the candidate is in this way sufficiently advanced, the third Trial awaits him. Here he has no feeling of a goal. Everything is left in his own hands. He finds himself in a situation where nothing prompts him to act. He must find his way quite alone, from out of himself. No persons or things are there to stimulate him to action. Nothing and nobody can now give him the strength he needs, but only he himself. Failure to find this strength in himself will very soon leave him standing where he stood before. Yet it must be said that only a few of those who have successfully passed the earlier Trials will fail to muster the necessary strength at this point. Either they will already have remained behind or they will succeed here also. All that is necessary is that the candidate shall be able quickly to come to terms with his own nature, for here he must find his 'higher self' in the truest sense of the word. He must instantly decide to listen in all things to the inspiration of the spirit. There is no time for doubt or hesitation. Every minute of delay would prove only that he is still unfit. Whatever keeps him from listening to the voice of the spirit must be boldly overcome. It is essential in this situation to have presence of mind, and the training at this stage is concerned with the full development of this quality. All inducements to act, or even to think, to which the candidate has previously been accustomed, now cease. In order not to remain inactive he must not lose himself, for only within his own being can he find the single firm point to which he can hold. Nobody who reads this without further acquaintance with these matters, should feel antipathy at this idea of being thrown back on oneself, for success in this Trial brings with it a feeling of supreme happiness.

At this stage, no less than at the others, everyday life is for many an occult training. Individuals who have reached the point of being able to come to a swift decision, without hesitation or much deliberation, when faced with tasks suddenly devolving upon them—for such individuals life itself is a training in this sense. There are situations where only immediate action will succeed. A person who can not only act instantly to ward off an imminent misfortune but has made this faculty of quick decision a permanent personal quality, has unconsciously attained the degree of maturity necessary for the third Trial. For what is essential at this stage is absolute presence of mind. In the occult schools this Trial is known as the 'Trial by Air' because while undergoing it the candidate can find no support either in the firm basis of external incentives or in what he has learnt from the patterns, tones and colours at the stages of Preparation and Enlightenment. He must find support solely in himself.

If this Trial has been successfully endured, the pupil may enter the 'Temple of higher Wisdom'. Very little more—only the barest indication—can be said about this. What has now to be carried out is often expressed by saying that the pupil must take an 'oath' to 'betray' nothing of the occult teachings. These expressions, 'oath' and 'betray', are inadequate and, to begin with, actually misleading. There is no question of an 'oath' in the ordinary sense of the word, but far rather of something learnt by *experience* at this stage of development. The candidate learns how to apply the occult teaching, how to place it in the service of humanity. He begins really to understand the world. It is not a question of witholding the higher truths, but far rather of presenting them in the right way and with the appropriate tact. The 'silence' he learns to keep is a quite different matter. He acquires this fine quality in regard to things of which he used previously to speak, especially in regard to the manner in which he spoke. He would be a bad Initiate who did not place all the mysteries he has experienced in the service of the world as far and as adequately as is possible. The only obstacle to communication in this field is lack of understanding by a recipient. Admittedly, the higher mysteries do not lend themselves to casual talk; but nobody who has reached the stage of development here described is actually 'forbidden' to say anything. No other individual, no being, imposes an 'oath' upon him with this intent. Everything is left to his own responsibility. He learns that in every situation he has to discover entirely through himself what he has to do. And the 'oath' means simply that he is fit to bear this responsibility.

If the candidate has come to be ready for the experiences described above, he is given what is called symbolically, the 'draught of forgetfulness'. This means that he is initiated into the secret of how to act without allowing himself to be continually disturbed by the lower memory. This is necessary for the Initiate, for he must at all times have full confidence in the immediate present. He must be able to wipe out the veil of memory which envelops man at every moment of his life. If I judge something that happens to me today according to what I experienced yesterday, I am exposed to a multitude of errors. Naturally this does not mean that experience gained in life should be disavowed. It should always be kept in mind as clearly as possible. But as an Initiate a man must have the capacity to judge every new experience exactly as it is and of letting it work upon him unobscured by anything from the past. I must be prepared at all times for the fact that every object or being can bring me some entirely new revelation. If I judge the new by the standard of the old, I am liable to error. Remembrance of past experiences will help me most by enabling me to see the new. If I had not had a particular experience, I might perhaps be blind to the essential character of the object or being before me. Experience, therefore, should serve the aim of envisioning the new, not of judging it by the standard of the old. In this respect the Initiate acquires very definite qualities. Many things that remain concealed from the uninitiated are thereby revealed to him.

The second 'draught' given to the Initiate is the 'draught of remembrance'. Through it he acquires the power to have higher mysteries always present in his soul. Ordinary memory would be unequal to this. We must become completely united with the higher truths. We must not only know them but be able, quite as a matter of course, to apply them in living action, just as we normally eat and drink. They must become practice, habit, inclination. There must be no need to keep thinking about them in the ordinary sense; they must come to expression through the man himself; they must flow through him like the currents of activity in his bodily organism. So will he raise himself in the spiritual sense more and more to the level to which Nature has brought him physically.

PRACTICAL ASPECTS

When an individual develops his feelings, thoughts and attitudes in the way described in the chapters dealing with the stages of Preparation, Enlightenment and Initiation, he brings about in his soul and spirit an organic membering similar to that brought about by Nature in his physical body. Before this development, soul and spirit are undifferentiated masses. The clairvoyant perceives them as interlacing, cloud-like spirals, dully gleaming with reddish, reddish-brown or even reddish-yellow tints; after development they begin to assume brilliant yellowish-green or greenish-blue colours and display regularity in their structure. This regularity, which leads to higher knowledge, is achieved when the pupil brings into his thoughts, feelings and attitudes a harmony such as that with which Nature has endowed his bodily functions, enabling him to hear, digest, breathe, speak and so on. The pupil learns gradually to breathe and see with the soul, to speak and hear with the spirit.

Some further practical aspects of the higher education of soul and spirit will be treated here in greater detail. They are of such a kind that anyone can give effect to them without taking account of other rules, and thereby be led some way into occult science.

A particular effort must be made to cultivate the quality

of *patience*. Every impulse of impatience has a paralysing, even a destructive, effect upon the higher faculties that slumber in the human being. Boundless insights into the higher worlds must not be expected from one day to the next, for then, as a rule, they will certainly not come. Contentment with the smallest achievement, calmness and composure, must more and more take root in the soul. It is quite understandable that the pupil will await results with impatience; but he will achieve nothing as long as he fails to master this impatience. Neither is it of any use to combat this impatience merely in the ordinary sense of the word, for then it only becomes so much the stronger. We then deceive ourselves about it and it takes root all the more firmly in the depths of the soul. It is only when we surrender ourselves again and again to a very definite thought, adopting it with every fibre of our being, that any result can be achieved. This thought is as follows: 'I must do everything I can to further the development of my soul and spirit, but I will wait quite calmly until higher Powers have found me worthy of Enlightenment.' If this thought becomes so powerful in the pupil that it grows into an actual trait of his character, he is treading the right path. This trait will then be evident even in his outer appearance. His gaze becomes steady, his movements more purposeful, his resolutions decisive, and everything that goes by the name of nervous tension, gradually disappears. Rules that seem trifling and insignificant must be taken into account. For example, suppose someone affronts us. Before training, our feeling would have been roused and directed against the offender; anger would have surged up from within us. In such a case, however, the thought that immediately arises in the mind of the pupil is: 'This insult does nothing to change my true value.' And then he does whatever has to be done to counter the insult with calmness and composure, not in anger. Naturally it is not a matter of passively accepting every insult, but of acting with the same calmness and assurance when countering an insult against our own person as we should if the insult had been directed against someone else on whose behalf we had the right to intervene. It must always be remembered that occult training is not carried out through crude, external processes, but through delicate, silent transformations in the life of feeling and thought.

Patience attracts the treasures of higher knowledge; impatience repels them. In the higher regions of existence nothing can be achieved by haste and unrest. Above all things, desire and craving must be silenced, for these are qualities of the soul from which all higher knowledge quietly withdraws with aversion. Valuable as all higher knowledge is, we must not crave for it if it is to come to us. He who wishes to have higher knowledge for his own sake will never attain it. And this requires above all that in the deepest depths of the soul a man shall be honest with himself. He must be under no illusion whatever concerning his own self. With inner truthfulness he must look fairly and squarely at his own faults, weaknesses and inadequacies. Directly you try to excuse to yourself any one of your weaknesses, you have laid a stone in the path that is to lead you upwards. You can remove such obstacles only by becoming clear about yourself. The only way to get rid of faults and failings is by recognising them for what they are. Every faculty is slumbering in the human soul and can be awakened. An individual can also improve his intellect and reason if he quietly and calmly brings home to himself why he is weak in this respect. Such self-knowledge is naturally difficult, for the temptation to be deluded about one's own nature is immeasurably great. Whoever makes a habit of being truthful with himself opens the portals to higher insight.

Every kind of curiosity must pass away from the pupil. He must rid himself as far as possible of the habit of asking questions about matters on which he wants information merely for the sake of satisfying his personal thirst for knowledge. He should ask only about matters which can help to make his own being a more effective servant of evolution. Nevertheless his delight in knowledge and his dedication to it should in no way be weakened. He should listen attentively to everything that serves this aim and seek every opportunity for practising this devotion.

Education of the life of *wishes* is especially necessary in the process of occult development. This does not mean that we should have no wishes: we must wish for anything that we are to attain, and a wish will always tend to be fulfilled if backed by a particular force. This force is derived from right knowledge. 'Do not wish at all before you have recognised what is right in any particular domain'—that is one of the golden rules for the pupil. The wise man first learns to know the laws of the world and then his wishes become powers which prove their efficacy.—The following example will bring this out. Many people wish to learn from their own vision something about their life before birth. Such a wish is altogether useless and leads to no result as long as the individual in question has not acquired through study of Spiritual Science a knowledge of the laws of the nature of the Eternal, in their subtlest, most intimate character. But if he has really acquired this knowledge and then wants to make further progress, his wish, ennobled and purified, will enable him to do so.

It is also useless to say: 'I want to survey my preceding life and to learn with that purpose in view.' We must far rather be able to abandon and eliminate this wish altogether and to learn, at the outset, with no such intention. We must cultivate feelings of joy and devotion for what we learn, with no thought of the above intention. For only so do we learn how to foster the corresponding wish in such a way that it brings fulfilment in its wake.

If I get angry or annoyed, I build a wall around myself in the soul-world, and the forces which should develop my eyes of soul cannot approach. If, for example, a person annoys me, a psychic current goes out from him into the soul-world. I cannot see this current as long as I am myself still capable of anger. My own anger conceals it from me. I must not, however, believe that when I no longer get angry I shall immediately have a psychic (astral) vision of the phenomenon. For this purpose an eye of the soul must develop in me. But the rudiments of such an organ are present in every human being. It remains ineffective as long as he is capable of anger. But neither is it immediately present when anger has been combated to a small extent. We must rather persevere in this combating of anger and patiently continue to do so; then one day we shall be aware that this eye of soul has opened.

Anger is certainly not the only failing to be combated in order to attain this end. Many become impatient or sceptical because they have fought against certain traits of soul for years, and yet clairvoyance has not developed. They will have cultivated certain qualities while allowing others to run riot. The gift of clairvoyance first manifests when all the qualities which hinder the emergence of the slumbering facilities are suppressed. Certainly the beginnings of vision (or of hearing) are present at an earlier stage; but these frail shoots are readily subject to errors of every kind, and moreover they easily die if they are not carefully tended.

Other traits which have to be combated as well as anger and irritability are timidity, superstition, prejudice, vanity and ambition, curiosity, eagerness to impart unnecessary information and the tendency to make distinctions among human beings according to the outer

97

characteristics of rank, sex, race, and so forth. In our time it will be extremely difficult for people to grasp that the combating of such traits has anything to do with enhancing the faculty of cognition. But every spiritual scientist knows that much more depends upon such things than upon the growth of intelligence and the practice of artificial exercises. Misunderstandings can very easily arise if people believe that they should be foolhardy because they ought to be fearless; that they should be blind to the differences in human beings because they ought to fight against prejudices connected with rank, race, and so forth. The fact is that we come to see things truly only when we are no longer steeped in prejudice. Even in a quite ordinary sense it is true that fear of some phenomenon will prevent me from judging it rightly; that racial prejudice will prevent me from seeing into a man's soul. It is this ordinary attitude that the pupil must carry further, with great delicacy and precision.

Every word spoken without having been thoroughly clarified in thought is a stone thrown in the way of esoteric training. And here something must be taken into consideration which can be explained only by an example. When something is said to me to which I have to reply, I must try hard to pay more heed to the speaker's opinion, feeling and even his prejudice, than to what I myself have to say at the moment about the matter in question. Here is indicated a delicate quality of tact, to the cultivation of which the pupil must dedicate himself. He must learn to

98

judge what importance it may have for the other person if he opposes the latter's opinion with his own. This does not mean that he should withhold his opinion. There is no question whatever of that. But he must listen to the other person with the closest possible attention and form his own reply out of what he has heard. In a case of this kind a particular thought occurs again and again to the pupil and he is treading the right path if this thought lives within him so strongly as to become a feature of his very character. This is the thought: 'The important point is not that my opinion differs from that of the other person, but that he will discover what is right out of himself if I contribute something towards it.' Thoughts of this kind shed a quality of gentleness over the character and behaviour of the pupil, and gentleness is one of the main factors in all esoteric training. Harshness scares away from around you the soul-forms which should awaken your inner eyes; gentleness clears away the obstacles and opens your inner eyes.

Together with gentleness, another trait will soon be developed in the soul of the pupil—that of quietly paying attention to all the delicate features in the soul-life around him while maintaining complete stillness within his own soul. If an individual has achieved this the emotions in his environment will work upon him in such a way that his own soul will grow, and in growing will develop an organic structure, just as a plant thrives in the sunlight. Gentleness and quiet inner patience open the soul to the soul-world, the spirit to the spirit-world.—'Persevere in quiet seclusion; close the senses to the messages they brought you before your training; bring to stillness all the thoughts which were in the habit of surging up and down within you; become inwardly still and silent, wait in patience, and then higher worlds will begin to fashion your eyes of soul and ears of spirit. You must not expect immediately to see and hear in the worlds of soul and spirit, for what you are doing is merely a contribution to the development of your higher senses. You will be able to use eyes of soul and ears of spirit only when you actually possess these senses. If you have persevered for a time in quiet seclusion, then go about your customary daily affairs, having imprinted deeply upon your mind this thought: some day, when I am ready, I shall attain what I am destined to attain. And strictly refrain from attempting by your own arbitrary will to draw any higher powers to yourself.'

These are instructions which every pupil receives from his teacher at the beginning of the path he is to tread. If he obeys them, he achieves his goal; if he does not obey them, all labour is in vain. But they are difficult only for one who lacks patience and perseverance. There are no obstacles other than those which a person places in his own path and can avoid if he so resolves. This must be continually emphasised, because many people form an entirely false idea of the difficulties of the esoteric path. In a certain sense it is easier to take the first steps along this path than to get the better of the commonest everyday difficulties of life without esoteric training. Apart from this, only such things as are attended by no dangers of any kind to the health of soul and body will be recommended here. There are other paths which lead more quickly to the goal, but what is here meant has nothing to do with them because they may have certain effects upon a man which an experienced occultist considers undesirable. As certain information about these paths is constantly finding its way to the public, express warning must be given against them. For reasons which only the initiated can understand, *these* paths can never be made publicly known in their real form. The fragments which come to light here and there can never lead to whole-some results but may easily undermine health, happiness and peace of mind. Anyone who does not want to entrust himself to dark, sinister Powers, of whose real nature and origin he can know nothing, had better have nothing to do with such things.

Something may still be said about the environment in which the exercises of esoteric training should be under-taken, for this is not without importance. Yet the circum-stances differ for almost every individual. Anyone who is practising the exercises in an environment imbued only with self-seeking interests, such as those which prevail in the modern struggle for existence, must be conscious of the fact that these interests are not without effect upon the development of his organs of soul. It is true that the inner laws of these organs are so powerful that no such influence can do decisive harm. A lily can never grow into a thistle, however inappropriate its environment; nor can the eye of the soul ever become anything other than it is destined to be, even when exposed to the self-seeking interests of modern cities. But under all circumstances it is beneficial if the pupil now and then surrounds himself with the restful peace, the intrinsic virtue and grace of Nature. Conditions are particularly favourable for one whose esoteric training can be pursued in the midst of the green world of plants, or among the sunny hills and the enchanted innocence of Nature. This environment draws out the inner organs in a harmony that can never be achieved in a modern city. An individual who at least during childhood was able to breathe the air perfumed by scent of fir-trees, to gaze at snowcapped mountain peaks and the peaceful life of wood-land creatures and insects, is more fortunate than the city-dweller. Yet no one who is obliged to live in a city should fail to provide his developing organs of soul and spirit with the nourishment afforded by the inspired teachings of spiritual research. He whose eyes cannot watch the woods turning green day by day in springtime should compensate by imbuing his heart and soul with the sublime teachings of the Bhagavad Gita, of St. John's Gospel, of St. Thomas à Kempis, and the descriptive findings of Spiritual Science. There are many paths to the summit of insight but a right choice is essential. Concerning these the esotericist can say much that will seem strange to the uninitiated. For example, someone may be very far advanced on the path; he may be at the very point where his eyes of soul and ears of spirit are about to open; and then he may be fortunate enough to journey over a calm or maybe a tempestuous sea and a veil falls away from the eyes of his soul; suddenly he becomes a seer. Another is equally at the point where this veil needs only to be loosened and this will come about through some drastic stroke of destiny. Upon another individual such a stroke might well have the effect of paralysing his strength and undermining his energy; for the esoteric pupil it becomes the cause of his Enlightenment. A third perseveres patiently for years without any perceptible result. Suddenly, while sitting peacefully in his room, spiritual light is all around him; the walls disappear, become transparent to his soul, and a new world stretches before his eyes that are now endowed with spiritual sight, or resounds in his ears that are now open to spiritual hearing.

THE CONDITIONS OF ESOTERIC
TRAINING

The conditions for embarking on esoteric training have not been arbitrarily determined. They arise from the essential nature of esoteric knowledge. Just as no one can become a painter who refuses to handle a paint brush, so, too, no one can receive esoteric training who is unwilling to fulfil the demands considered necessary by teachers. Fundamentally speaking, the teacher can give nothing except advice, and everything he says should be accepted in this sense. He has already passed through the preparatory paths to knowledge of the higher worlds and knows from experience what is necessary. It rests entirely upon the *free will* of each individual whether he chooses to tread the same paths or not. Were anyone to demand that a teacher should admit him to esoteric training without his having fulfilled the conditions, this would be equivalent to saying: Teach me how to paint but do not ask me to handle a paint brush. The teacher can offer nothing unless the would-be recipient comes to meet him of his own free will. But it must be emphasised that a general wish for higher knowledge is not sufficient. Many people, of course, will have this wish, but nothing can be achieved by it alone, as long as the special conditions attached to esoteric training are not accepted. This point should be considered by those who complain that esoteric training is not going to be easy for them. Failure or unwillingness to fulfil the strict conditions must for the time being entail the abandonment of esoteric training. True, the conditions are strict, but they are not rigid, because the fulfilment of them not only should be, but actually must be, a free deed.

If this fact is overlooked, the conditions of esoteric training may easily seem to involve a coercion of the soul or the conscience; for the training is based upon development of the *inner* life and the teacher must therefore give corresponding advice. But nothing that is required to spring from free decision can be interpreted as compulsion. If someone asks the teacher: Tell me your secrets but leave me with my wonted emotions, feelings and thoughts—that is an unrealistic demand. The person simply wants to satisfy his curiosity and desire for knowledge. With this attitude of mind, higher knowledge can never be attained.

We will now consider in sequence the conditions to be observed by the pupil. It must be emphasised that the *complete* fulfilment of any one of these conditions is not demanded, but only the endeavour to fulfil them. No one can wholly fulfil the conditions, but everyone can set out on the path towards their fulfilment. All that matters is the effort of will, the setting of the mind to enter upon this path.

The first condition is that heed should be paid to the furtherance of bodily and spiritual *health*. Health does not, of course, primarily depend upon the individual; but everyone can make the effort to improve in this respect. Healthy knowledge can come only from healthy human beings. In esoteric training an unhealthy individual is not rejected, but it must be demanded of the pupil that he has the will to lead a healthy life. In this respect he must achieve the greatest possible independence. The well-meaning advice of others, given—mostly unsought—to everyone, is as a rule quite superfluous. Each individual must endeavour to take care of himself. In a physical respect it will be more a matter of warding off harmful influences than of anything else. In order to carry out our duties we must often undertake things that are not conducive to our health. When it is right to do so, a man must decide to give preference to duty rather than to the care of health. But just think how many things can be given up with a little goodwill. Duty must in many cases be more important than health, often indeed more important than life itself; but for the esoteric pupil this should never apply to pleasure. For him, pleasure can be only a means towards health and life. And here, above all, everyone must be honest and truthful with himself. It is useless to lead an ascetic life when the underlying motives are the same as in other enjoyments. Someone may derive satisfaction from asceticism, as someone else does from wine-drinking, but he cannot hope that asceticism of this kind will help him to attain higher knowledge. Many ascribe to their station in life everything that apparently prevents them from making progress in this respect. They say: 'In the present conditions of my life I cannot develop.' For other reasons it may be desirable for many to change their stations in life, but no one need do so for the purpose of esoteric training. He need do only as much as is possible, whatever his position, to further the health of his body and soul. Every kind of work can be of service to mankind as a whole; and it is a much greater achievement of the soul to realise how necessary for mankind is a trivial, perhaps even an unpleasant employment, than to think: 'This work is not good enough for me; I am destined for something better.' Of special importance for the pupil is the striving for a completely healthy mind. An unhealthy life of feeling and thought will in every case obstruct the paths to higher knowledge. Clear, calm thinking, stability of feeling and emotion are the fundamentals here. Nothing should be farther from the pupil than any tendency to a fancy-ridden, excitable life, to nervous tension, exaltation and fanaticism. He should acquire a healthy outlook on all circumstances in life; he should find his bearings in life with assurance; he should quietly let things work upon him and speak to him. He should be at pains to meet the demands of life in all necessary directions. All exaggerated, one-sided tendencies in his judgment and feeling should be avoided. If this condition were not fulfilled he would find his way into worlds of his own imagination instead of higher worlds; instead of truth, his own pet opinions would assert themselves. It is better for a pupil to be 'matter-of-fact' than excitable and full of fancies.

The second condition is to feel oneself a member of humanity as a whole. A great deal is included in the fulfilment of this condition, but each individual can fulfil it only in his own way. If I am a teacher and a pupil is not what I would wish him to be, I should not direct my feeling primarily against him but against myself. I should feel at one with my pupil to the extent of asking myself: 'Is his shortcoming not the result of my own action?' Instead of directing my feeling against him, I shall then far rather reflect upon how I should myself behave in order that he may in future be better able to satisfy my expectations. Such an attitude gradually brings about a change in the whole of a man's way of thinking. This holds good in all things, the smallest and the greatest alike. With this attitude of mind I shall see a criminal, for example, differently. I suspend my judgment and say to myself: 'I am a human being just as he is. The education which circumstances made possible for me may alone have saved me from his fate.' I shall then certainly arrive at the thought that this human brother would have become a different man if the teachers who took pains with me had bestowed the same care upon him. I shall reflect that something was given to me which was withheld from him, that I owe my good fortune to the circumstance that it was withheld from him. And then it will no longer be difficult for me to think that I am only a member of humanity as a whole and share responsibility for everything that occurs. This does not imply that such a thought should be immediately translated into outer agitation. It should rather be tended in stillness within the soul. Then, quite gradually, it will set its mark upon the outward bearing of a man. In such matters each one has to begin by reforming himself. It is of no avail to make general demands of humanity in the sense of the foregoing thoughts. It is easy to decide what men ought to be; but the pupil works in the depths, not on the surface. It would therefore be quite wrong to connect the demand of the esoteric teacher indicated here with any external, let alone political, demand with which spiritual training can have nothing to do. Political agitators 'know', as a rule, what to 'demand' of other people; but they seldom speak of demands on themselves.

The third condition in esoteric training is directly connected with what has been said above. The pupil must be able to work his way to the realisation that his thoughts and feelings are as important for the world as his actions. He must recognise that it is just as harmful to hate a fellow-being as to strike him. The knowledge then comes to me that when I strive to improve myself, I accomplish something not only for myself but also for the world. The world derives as much benefit from my unsullied feelings and thoughts as from my good conduct. As long as I cannot believe in this importance of my inner life for the world I am not fit to be an esoteric pupil. I shall be imbued with the right belief in the significance of my inner self, of my soul, when I work at it as though it were at least as real as anything external. I must come to admit that every feeling has as real an effect as an action of my hand.

Herewith the fourth condition is already indicated: to become convinced that the real being of man lies not in the outer world but in the inner world. Anyone who regards himself as a product merely of the outer world, as an outcome of the physical world, can achieve nothing in esoteric training, for to feel oneself a being of soul and spirit is its very basis. Anyone who acquires this feeling is able to distinguish between inner duty and outward success. He learns to rcognise that the one cannot be directly measured by the other. The esoteric pupil must find the right mean between what is prescribed by external conditions and the conduct he recognises as right for himself. He should not force upon his environment anything for which it can have no understanding; but he must also be quite free from the desire to do only what his environment will accept. Recognition of the truths for which he stands must be sought *only* in the voice of his own soul, with its genuine striving for knowledge. But he must learn as much as he possibly can from his environment in order to discover what will benefit those around him and be useful to them. In this way he will develop what is known in Spiritual Science as 'spiritual balance'. An 'open heart' for the needs of the outer world lies on one of the scales and 'inner resoluteness and unswerving endurance' on the other.

This points to the fifth condition: steadfastness in carrying out a resolution once it is taken. Nothing should induce the pupil to deviate from a resolution he has taken, except the insight that he is wrong. Every resolution is a force, and even if this force does not have immediate success at the point where it is applied, nevertheless it works on in its own way. Success is decisive only if an action arises from desire. But all such actions are worthless in face of the higher world. There, love for an action is alone decisive. Everything that impels the pupil to action should find expression in love. Then he will never weary in his efforts to translate a resolution into deed, however often he may fail. And in this way he reaches the stage of not waiting to see the outward effect of his deeds, but of being content with what they are in themselves. He will learn to offer up his deeds, even his whole being, to the world, no matter how the world may receive his sacrifice. Anyone who wishes to become an esoteric pupil must resolve to be ready for a life of sacrifice.

A sixth condition is the development of a feeling of thankfulness for everything that falls to man's lot. We must realise that our own existence is a gift from the whole universe. How much is needed in order that each one of us may receive and sustain our existence! How much do we not owe to nature and to other human beings! Those who wish for esoteric training must incline to such thoughts. He who is incapable of lending himself to them is also incapable of developing the all-embracing love that is necessary for the attainment of higher knowledge. Something that I do not love cannot reveal itself to me. And every revelation must fill me with thankfulness, for I am the richer for it.

All these conditions must unite in the seventh: to grasp life constantly in the way demanded by these conditions. The pupil is thus enabled to give his life a uniform character. All his ways of expressing himself will be brought into harmony with each other and no longer be contradictory. He will be prepared for the inner tranquillity he must achieve during the first steps of esoteric training.

Anyone who has the sincere and genuine will to fulfil these conditions may decide to undertake esoteric training. He will then be ready to follow the advice indicated above. Much of this advice may appear superficial to many people and they will perhaps say that they had expected the training to take less strict forms. But everything inward must come to expression outwardly. And as little as a picture is really there when it exists only in the mind of the artist, as little can any esoteric training have no outward expression. Disregard for strict forms is shown only by those who do not know that the internal must come to expression in the external. True, it is the *spirit* of a thing that matters, not the form; but just as the form without the spirit is null and void, so would the spirit remain inactive if it did not create a form for itself.

The conditions are designed to render the pupil strong enough to meet the further demands that his training will unavoidably make upon him. If he fails to fulfil these conditions, he will be hesitant and apprehensive when faced with every new demand. He will lack the faith in man that is necessary for him. All striving for truth must be founded upon faith in and true love for man. This must be its foundation, but not its origin: striving for truth can flow only from the soul's own power. And the love of man must widen gradually into love for all beings; indeed for all existence. Anyone who fails to fulfil the above conditions will lack the genuine love for everything that upbuilds and creates, and the inclination to refrain from all destructiveness. The pupil must become a person who never destroys anything for the sake of destruction, not only in his actions but also in his words, feelings and thoughts. He must delight in growth, in development, and he must lend his hand to destruction only when he is also able, through and from out of destruction, to promote new life. This does not mean that he must look on passively while evil runs riot; but rather that even in what is evil he must look for those aspects through which he may transform it into good. He will then see more and more clearly that evil and imperfection are best combated by the creation of the perfect and the good. The pupil knows that out of empty nothingness, nothing can be created, but also that the imperfect can be transformed into the perfect. Anyone who develops within himself the propensity for creative activity will soon find himself capable of dealing with evil in the right way.

Anyone who embarks upon esoteric training must realise that its purpose is to build, not to destroy; the pupil should therefore bring with him the will for sincere and devoted work, not for criticism and destructiveness. He must be capable of devotion, for he has to learn what he does not yet know; he should have reverence for whatever discloses itself to him. Work and devotion are the fundamental demands made upon the pupil. Many a one will have to realise that he is making no progress in his training, although in his own opinion he is indefatigably active. The reason is that he has not rightly grasped the nature of work and devotion. Work undertaken for the sake of success will be the least successful, and learning pursued without devotion will bring the least progress. Love of the work itself, not of success—this alone leads to progress. And if the learner is trying to develop healthy thinking and sound judgment, he need not vitiate his devotion through doubt and distrust.

Nobody need be reduced to servile dependence by listening to information with quiet reverence and attention, instead of at once countering it with his own opinion. Those who have acquired a certain amount of higher knowledge know that they owe everything to quiet attentiveness and patient reflection, not to wilful personal judgment. We should always bear in mind that there is no need to learn anything we can already judge. If, therefore, we want *only* to judge, we can learn nothing more. In esoteric training, however, it is learning that matters. We should desire with heart and soul to be learners. If there is something we cannot understand, it is better not to judge at all than to judge adversely. Understanding can be left until later. The higher we climb the steps of knowledge, the more necessary is this quiet, reverent listening. All perception of truth, all life and action in the world of the spirit, are subtle and delicate in comparison with the functions of the ordinary intellect and the business of life in the physical world. The wider our horizon becomes, the more delicate are the activities we have to undertake. It is because of this that people arrive at such different 'opinions' and 'points of view' regarding higher spheres. But there is in reality one and only one opinion regarding higher truths, and this one opinion is within reach of everyone who through work and devotion has risen to the stage where he can actually behold the truth. A view that differs from the one true view can be arrived at only when someone, insufficiently prepared, judges in accordance with his pet ideas, his habitual thoughts, and so forth. Just as there is only one valid opinion about a mathematical theorem, so is it with the things of the higher worlds. But before anyone can reach an 'opinion' of the kind, he must have undergone a proper preparation for doing so. If this were duly recognised, the conditions made by the teacher in esoteric training would surprise no one. It is absolutely correct that truth and the higher life abide in every human soul and that each individual can and must find them for himself. But they lie deeply buried and can be brought up from the depths only after all obstacles have been cleared away. Only those with experience can advise how this may be done. Spiritual

Science gives such advice. It forces no truth on anyone proclaims no dogma; but it shows a way. It is true that everyone could also find this way unaided, but perhaps only after many incarnations. The way is shortened by esoteric training. Through it a man can more quickly reach a point where he can co-operate in those worlds where the salvation and evolution of man are furthered through spiritual activity.

This concludes the indications which are to be given for the time being on achieving experience of higher worlds. In the next chapter, and in continuation of what has been said above, it will be shown how this process of development affects the higher members of man's constitution (the soul-organism or astral body and the spirit or thought-body). New light will thereby be shed on the indications here given and it will be possible to penetrate more deeply into them.

SOME EFFECTS OF INITIATION

One of the fundamental principles of true occult science is that whoever devotes himself to it should do so with full consciousness; he should undertake nothing, practise nothing, without knowledge of the effect produced. When giving advice or instruction, a teacher of occult science will always explain to those in search of higher knowledge the effects that will be produced on body, soul or spirit if his instructions are followed.

Some of the effects produced upon the soul of the pupil will here be indicated, for such knowledge is indispensable to anyone who with full consciousness undertakes the exercises leading to knowledge of the higher worlds. Only such an individual is an esoteric pupil in the true sense. In genuine esoteric training all groping in the dark is strictly discouraged. Anyone who is unwilling to pursue this training with open eyes may become a medium; he cannot become a clairvoyant in the sense of occult science.

If the exercises described in the preceding sections (on the acquisition of supersensible knowledge), are practised rightly, certain changes take place in the so-called soul-organism. The latter is perceptible only to the clairvoyant. It can be compared to a more or less spiritually and psychically luminous cloud, in the centre of which the physical body is found.* In this soul-organism, impulses, desires, passions, ideas and so forth become visible spiritually. Sensual desires, for example, create the impression of a dark red radiation, with a definite form. A pure and noble thought has its expression in a reddish-violet radiation. The clear-cut concept of a logical thinker is felt as a yellowish figure with sharply defined outlines. The confused thought of a muddled mind appears as a figure with vague outlines. The thoughts of people with one-sided, obstinate views appear sharply outlined, but immobile, while the thoughts of personalities who are open to the views of others are seen to have mobile, changing outlines, and so on and so forth.†

The further the individual advances in his inner development, the more clearly differentiated in structure will his soul-organism become. In a man with an undeveloped life of soul this organism is confused, relatively formless. But even in a confused soul-organism the clairvoyant can perceive a form which stands out distinctly from its

* A description will be found in the book *Theosophy* (pp. 22-34 in the 1965 English edition).

† In all the following descriptions it must be remembered that 'seeing' a colour means *spiritual seeing*. When it is said with clairvoyant consciousness: 'I see a red colour', this means: 'In the sphere of spirit-and-soul I have an experience equivalent to the physical experience arising from an impression of the colour red.' This mode of expression is used here only because in such a case it is perfectly natural for clairvoyant consciousness to say: 'I see a red colour.' If this point is overlooked, a mere colour-vision may easily be mistaken for a genuine clairvoyant experience.

environment. It extends from the interior of the head to the middle of the physical body. It appears as a kind of independent body, possessing certain organs. These organs, now to be considered, are perceived spiritually near the following parts of the physical body: the first between the eyes, the second in the neighbourhood of the larynx, the third in the region of the heart; the fourth near the so-called pit of the stomach; the fifth and sixth are situated in the abdomen. These organs are called by occultists, 'wheels' (chakrams) or also 'lotus-flowers'. They are so called because of their likeness to wheels or flowers, but it must of course be clearly understood that such expressions are not much apter than when the lobes of the lungs are called 'wings'. Just as there is no question of 'wings' in the case of the lungs, so in the case of the lotus-flowers the expression must be taken as a figurative comparison. In undeveloped persons these lotus-flowers are dark in colour, motionless and inert. In the clairvoyant, however, they are in movement, and shot through with luminous shades of colour. Something of the kind applies to the medium though with a difference; but we will not go further into that here.

When a pupil begins his exercises, the lotus-flowers become brighter, and later on they begin to revolve. When this happens, the faculty of clairvoyance begins to function. For these 'flowers' are the sense-organs of the soul* and

* What was said in the previous footnote about the 'seeing of colours' is applicable also to these perceptions of 'revolutions'; indeed of the lotus-flowers themselves.

their revolution is an expression of the fact that super-sensible perception has been achieved. No one can perceive anything supersensible until his astral senses have developed in this way.

The spiritual organ situated near the larynx makes it possible to perceive clairvoyantly the character of another being's thoughts, and also to gain deeper insight into the true laws of natural phenomena. The organ situated near the heart brings clairvoyant knowledge of the sentiments and outlook of other souls. When developed, this organ also makes it possible to recognise certain deeper forces in animals and plants. By means of the organ in the so-called pit of the stomach, knowledge is acquired of the faculties and talents of souls; by its means the part played in the household of Nature by animals, plants, stones, metals, atmospheric phenomena and so on can be discerned.

The organ in the vicinity of the larynx has sixteen 'petals' or 'spokes'; the one in the region of the heart has twelve, and the organ near the pit of the stomach, ten.

Now certain activities of the soul are connected with the development of these organs, and anyone who carries out these activities in a quite specific way contributes something to the development of the corresponding spiritual sense-organs. In the case of the sixteen-petalled lotus-flower, eight of its sixteen petals were developed during an earlier stage of man's evolution, in a remote past. Man himself contributed nothing to *this* development; it was a gift from Nature, at a time when his consciousness was still in a dim, dreamlike condition. At that stage of evolution the petals were also active, but in a way compatible only with that dim state of consciousness. As consciousness then became clearer and brighter, the petals darkened and their activity ceased. Man himself can develop the other eight petals by exercises consciously practised. Thereby the whole lotus-flower becomes luminous and mobile. The acquisition of certain faculties depends upon the development of each one of the sixteen petals. Yet, as already indicated, only eight of them can be developed consciously; the other eight then appear of their own accord.

The development proceeds in the following way. The pupil must pay careful attention to certain functions of the soul which he generally carries out carelessly and inattentively. There are eight such functions. The first is the way in which ideas are acquired. In this connection a man usually allows himself to be led entirely by chance. He hears this and that, sees one thing or another, and forms his ideas accordingly. As long as this continues his sixteen-petalled lotus-flower remains inoperative. Only when he takes his self-education in hand in this respect does it become operative. He must watch over his ideas or mental concepts. Every idea should be of significance for him; he should see in it a definite message instructing him concerning things of the outer world, and he should not be satisfied with ideas devoid of such significance. He must direct his mental life in such a way that it becomes a faithful mirror of the outer world. He should endeavour to banish incorrect ideas from his soul.

The second of these functions is concerned with a similar control of resolutions. The pupil should not resolve upon even the most insignificant act without well-founded and thorough consideration. All thoughtless and meaningless actions shuld be foreign to his nature. He should have well-considered grounds for everything he does, and should abstain from everything for which no such grounds exist.

The third function has to do with speech. Only such words as have sense and meaning should come from the pupil's lips. All talking for the sake of talking diverts him from his path. He should avoid the usual kind of conversation, with its indiscriminate, haphazard chatter. This does not mean shutting himself off from communication with his fellow-men, but he should bring increasing significance into his words. He is ready to talk with everyone, but he does so thoughtfully and always with consideration. He never speaks without grounds for what he says. He tries to use neither too many nor too few words.

The fourth function is the regulation of *outer* action. The pupil tries to adjust his actions in such a way that they harmonise with those of his fellow-men and with happenings in his environment. He refrains from actions which are disturbing to others or at variance with what is going on around him. He tries to direct his actions in such a way that they are membered harmoniously into his surroundings, his position in life, and so on. When an external motive prompts him to act, he considers how he can best respond. When the impulse proceeds from himself, he weighs with utmost care the effects of his activity.

The fifth function includes the management of the whole of his life. The pupil endeavours to live in conformity with both Nature and Spirit. Never over-hasty, he is never indolent. Excessive activity and laziness are equally alien to him. He looks upon life as a means for work and orders himself accordingly. He regulates his habits, the care of his health and so on, in such a way as to yield a harmonious life.

The sixth function concerns human endeavour. The pupil puts his capacities and proficiency to the test and conducts himself in the light of such self-knowledge. He tries to avoid everything that is beyond his powers but also to omit nothing that is within their scope. On the other hand, he sets before himself aims connected with the ideals and the great duties of a human being. He does not thought-lessly regard himself as a wheel in the vast machinery of mankind but tries to comprehend his tasks and to look beyond everyday affairs. He endeavours to fulfil his obligations more and more thoroughly.

The seventh function is concerned with the endeavour to learn from life as much as possible. Nothing comes to the pupil's notice without giving him occasion to gather experience of value for his life. If he has performed anything wrongly or imperfectly, this is an incentive for him to accomplish something of the same kind correctly or perfectly later on. When he sees others acting he observes them with the same end in view. He tries to gather a rich store of experiences and to turn to it constantly for counsel. And he does nothing without looking back on experiences which can be of help to him in his decisions and actions.

Finally, the eighth function is that the pupil must from time to time take prudent counsel with himself, practise introspection, sink into himself, form and test the basic principles of his life, survey in thought the sum-total of his knowledge, weigh his duties, reflect about the content and aim of life, and so on. All these things have been mentioned in the preceding chapters; they are enumerated here merely in connection with the development of the sixteen-petalled lotus-flower. If these principles are practised, this lotus-flower will become more and more perfect, for it is upon such practices that the development of clairvoyance depends. The better a man's thoughts and speech harmonise with occurrences in the outer world, the more quickly will this faculty develop. Whoever thinks or speaks an untruth destroys something in the seed of the sixteen-petalled lotus-flower. Truthfulness, sincerity and integrity are in this connection upbuilding forces; mendacity, deceitfulness and dishonesty are destructive. The pupil must realise, however, that what matters here is not only the 'good intention' but the actual deed. If I think or say anything that does not conform with reality, I destroy something in my spiritual organ, even though I believe my intention to be entirely good. It is the same as when a child burns itself by putting its hand into the fire, even though this was done all unknowingly.

The regulation of all these activities of the soul in the manner described enables the sixteen-petalled lotus-flower to ray out in glorious colours and sets it into orderly movement. Yet it must be noted that the faculty of clairvoyance cannot arise before the soul has reached a definite degree of development. This faculty does not emerge as long as it is irksome for the pupil to conduct his life in accordance with these principles. He is still unfit as long as the activities described above demand special attention from him. The first traces of clairvoyance do not appear until an individual has reached the point of being able to live habitually in the way indicated. These tasks must be no longer irksome, but a natural way of life. There must be no need for a man to be continually watching and urging himself to live in this way. Everything must have become habit.

There are certain instructions whereby the development of the sixteen-petalled lotus-flower is brought about in a different way. All such methods are rejected by true occult science, for they lead to the shattering of bodily health and to moral ruin. They are easier to follow than the method here described. This method is protracted and laborious, but it leads to the true goal and cannot but strengthen morality.

The distorted development of a lotus-flower leads not only to illusions and fantastic conceptions, if a certain faculty of clairvoyance ensues, but also to aberrations and instability in ordinary life. Such a development may be the cause of timidity, envy, vanity, haughtiness, wilfulness and the like in a person who was hitherto free from all these characteristics. It has been said that eight of the sixteen petals of this lotus-flower were already developed in a remote past and that these reappear of themselves in the course of esoteric training. All the effort and attention of the pupil must be devoted to the remaining eight. Faulty training may easily result in the reappearance of the earlier petals alone, while those to be developed remain inert. This will especially be the case if in the training too little attention is paid to logical, rational thinking. It is of supreme importance that the pupil should be a discerning and clear-thinking human being, and important also that he should aim at the greatest clarity of speech. People who begin to have some inkling of supersensible matters are apt to wax talkative on this subject, thereby retarding their proper development. The less one talks about these matters, the better. No one should speak about them until he has achieved a certain degree of clarity.

At the beginning of their instruction, pupils are as a rule astonished to find how little curiosity someone spiritually trained will show towards any accounts they give of their own experiences. Much the healthiest thing would be for them to remain entirely silent about their experiences and simply to say how far they have been successful or un-successful in carrying out their exercises or in following the instructions given them. For anyone who is spiritually trained can estimate their progress by means quite other than their own communications. The eight petals of the sixteen-petalled lotus-flower are always somewhat hardened as the result of such communications, whereas they should be kept pliant and supple. An example, taken for the sake of clarity not from the supersensible world but from ordinary life, will explain this. Suppose I hear a piece of news and immediately form an opinion about it. Shortly afterwards I receive some further news which does not tally with the previous information. I am thereby obliged to recast the judgment I had already formed. This has an unfavourable influence on my sixteen-petalled lotus-flower. It would have been quite different if in the first place I had withheld my judgment of the whole affair and remained silent, both inwardly in thoughts and outwardly in words, until I had reliable grounds for forming my judgment. Caution in forming and voicing judgments gradually becomes a special characteristic of the pupil. On the other hand his receptivity increases for impressions and experiences which he allows silently to pass over him in order to create as many points of approach as possible when the time comes to make his judgment. Bluish-red and rosy-pink shades colour the petals of the sixteen-petalled lotus-flower as the result of such caution, whereas, in the opposite case, dark red and orange shades appear.*

* Many will recognise in the conditions for the development of the sixteen-petalled lotus-flower the instructions given by the

The twelve-petalled lotus-flower, situated in the region of the heart, is similarly formed. Half its petals, too, were already in existence and active in a past stage of evolution. Hence these six petals need not be definitely developed in esoteric training; they appear of themselves and begin to revolve when the pupil works at the other six. Here again, in order to promote this development he must consciously give a particular direction to certain soul-activities.

It must be clearly understood that each of the spiritual or soul-organs transmits perceptions of a different character. The sixteen-petalled lotus-flower perceives forms. The kind of thoughts harboured by a soul and the laws governing a phenomenon of Nature appear to the sixteen-petalled lotus-flower as figures—not rigid, motionless figures but mobile forms filled with life. The clairvoyant in whom this sense is developed can discern for every trend of thought and for every law of Nature, forms through which they are expressed. A revengeful thought, for example, clothes itself in an arrow-like, jagged form, while a kindly thought often has the form of an opening flower, and so on. Clear-cut, meaningful thoughts are regular, symmetrical in form; confused thoughts have wavy outlines.

Buddha to his disciples for the 'Path'. There is no question here of teaching Buddhism, but of describing conditions for development which are the outcome of Spiritual Science itself. The fact that these conditions tally with certain teachings of the Buddha is no reason for not finding them true *in themselves*.

Quite different perceptions are received through the twelve-petalled lotus-flower. These perceptions may be likened approximately to warmth and cold, as applied to the soul. A clairvoyant possessed of this faculty feels this warmth or coldness of soul streaming from the forms perceived through the sixteen-petalled lotus-flower. If he had developed the sixteen- and not the twelve-petalled lotus-flower, he would perceive a kindly thought, for instance, only in the form described above, whereas a clairvoyant in whom both senses have developed will also notice what can be described as soul-warmth streaming from the thought. In esoteric training, however, the one sense is never developed without the other, so that the example above is given simply for the sake of clarity. Through the development of the twelve-petalled lotus-flower a deep understanding of processes of Nature begins to arise in the clairvoyant. Soul-warmth streams out from everything involved in growth and development; everything that is involved in decay, destruction, decline, gives an impression of coldness.

The development of this sense is furthered in the following way. The first requirement to which the pupil applies himself is the regulation of the sequence of his thoughts (the so-called *control of thoughts*). Just as the sixteen-petalled lotus-flower is developed by cultivating thoughts that have genuine significance, the twelve-petalled lotus-flower develops through inner control of the course taken by thoughts. Thoughts that dart hither and thither like will-o'-the-wisps, and are linked together without any logical or rational sequence but purely by chance, destroy the form of this lotus-flower. The more logically one thought follows upon the other, the more everything illogical is set aside, the more surely does this spiritual sense-organ assume its appropriate form. If the pupil hears illogical thoughts being expressed, he immediately lets a correct version pass through his mind. He should not withdraw in a loveless way from an environment that may be replete with illogicalities, in order to further his own development. Neither should he feel urged immediately to correct all the illogical thoughts that are being voiced around him. Far rather will he, quietly and inwardly, bring them into an order that makes logical sense. And he endeavours always to keep to this course in his own thoughts.

To bring a like logical sequence into his actions is the second requirement (*control of actions*). All inconsistency, all disharmony in action conduces to the ruin of the lotus-flower here concerned. When the pupil has performed some deed, he adapts his next action in such a way that it follows logically from the first. A person whose action today is at variance with that of yesterday will never develop the organ here being characterised.

The third requirement is the cultivation of *endurance*. The pupil is impervious to all influences that would divert him from the goal he has set himself, as long as he can regard this goal as right. Obstacles are a challenge to him to overcome them, never reasons for delaying his progress.

The fourth requirement is forbearance (*tolerance*) towards men, other beings and also circumstances. The pupil suppresses all superfluous criticism of whatever is imperfect, evil and wrong and tries rather to understand everything that comes to him. Just as the sun does not withdraw its light from the wrong and the evil, he too does not refuse them intelligent sympathy. Should some adversity befall him, he does not indulge in adverse criticism but accepts what necessity has brought him and endeavours as best he can to turn things to good. He does not look at the opinions of others merely from his own standpoint but tries to put himself into their position.

The fifth requirement is *impartiality* towards all that comes to meet him in life. In this connection we speak of 'faith' or 'trust'. The pupil meets every man and every other being with this trust and lets it inspire his actions. When anything is communicated to him, he never says to himself: 'I don't believe it because it contradicts the opinion I have hitherto held.' Far rather he is ready at every moment to test and rectify his views and opinions. He remains always receptive to everything that approaches him and he trusts in the effectiveness of what he undertakes. He banishes faint-heartedness and scepticism. If he has a purpose in view, he also has faith in its power. A hundred failures cannot rob him of this faith. It is the 'faith that can move mountains'.

The sixth requirement is the acquisition of a certain equilibrium in life (*equanimity*). The pupil endeavours to retain his equanimity in the face of joy or sorrow. He breaks himself of the habit of fluctuating between the seventh heaven of jubilation and the depths of despair. Misfortune and danger, fortune and advancement alike, find him ready armed.

The reader of spiritual-scientific literature will recognise in the qualities here described the 'six attributes' which the aspirant for Initiation must develop in himself. The intention here has been to show their connection with the organ of soul known as the twelve-petalled lotus-flower. Here, again, occult training can give special instructions which will bring this lotus-flower to fruition, but here, too, the regularity of its form depends upon the development of the qualities enumerated. If this development is neglected, the organ will become a caricature of itself. In this case, if a certain faculty of clairvoyance were to develop, the qualities in question would turn to the bad instead of to the good. A person may become very intolerant, faint-hearted, at variance with his environment; he may, for instance, become sensitive to the sentiments of others, and for this reason shun them or hate them. This may even go so far that by reason of the inner coldness overwhelming him he cannot bear to listen to opinions contrary to his own, or he may behave in an antagonistic manner.

The development of this lotus-flower may be accelerated if, in addition to all that has here been said, certain other injunctions are observed which can be imparted to the pupil only by word of mouth. The instructions given here do, however, lead to genuine esoteric training. The regulation of life in the way described can also be helpful to an individual who cannot or is unwilling to undergo esoteric training. For it does not fail to produce an effect upon the soul-organism, even though slowly. For the esoteric pupil, the observance of these fundamental principles is indispensable. Should he attempt an esoteric training without conforming to them, he would inevitably enter the higher worlds with inadequate organs of thought, and instead of recognising the truth he would be subject only to deceptions and illusions. He might become clairvoyant in a certain sense, but fundamentally he would be the victim of even greater blindness than before. Formerly he at least stood firmly in the physical world; but now he sees behind this physical world and loses his way in it before acquiring a firm footing in a higher world. All power of distinguishing truth from error may fail him and he may lose all sense of direction in life. That is why patience is so necessary in these matters. It must always be remembered that the instructions given in Spiritual Science must not outrun the pupil's complete willingness to develop the lotus-flowers in an orderly way. If the lotus-flowers were brought to maturity before they had quietly developed their proper *forms*, sheer caricatures would result. For while the special instructions given in Spiritual Science activate the *maturing* process, the *form* is imparted by the manner of life described above.

An inner training of a specially delicate kind is necessary

for the development of the ten-petalled lotus-flower, for it is here a matter of learning to have conscious control of the sense-impressions themselves. This is particularly important for the incipient clairvoyant. Only by this means can he avoid a source of countless illusions and spiritual fantasies. As a rule a man does not in the least realise by what factors his sudden thoughts and memories are controlled or how they are evoked. Consider the following case. Someone is travelling by train; his mind is occupied with a certain thought which suddenly takes a different turn. He remembers an experience he had years ago and weaves it into his present thought. But he is quite unaware that in looking through the carriage window he had caught sight of a person who resembled someone closely connected with the remembered experience. He is not conscious of what he actually saw, but only of the effect it produced, and so he believes it all came to him spontaneously. How much in life occurs in that sort of way! What a large part is played in our lives by things we have experienced and read about without consciously realising the connections! Someone, for instance, cannot bear a certain colour, but does not realise that this is because a teacher who was unkind to him many years ago wore a coat of that colour. Innumerable illusions are based upon such associations. Many things impress themselves upon the soul without coming into the sphere of consciousness. The following may happen. Someone reads in the newspaper about the death of a well-known person and firmly claims to have had a 'presentiment' of it the day before, although he has not heard or seen anything that might have given rise to such a thought. And indeed it is quite true that the thought occurred to him 'yesterday', as though of its own accord, that this particular person would die. But one point escaped his attention: two or three hours before this thought occurred to him 'yesterday', he went to visit an acquaintance. A newspaper was lying on the table; he did not read it, but unconsciously his eye fell on the news that the person in question was dangerously ill. He had not been conscious of the impression he received, but its effect was the 'presentiment'.

Reflection on these things brings home to us what a deep source of illusion and fantasy lies in such associations. And this source must be nullified by anyone who desires to develop his ten-petalled lotus-flower. Deeply hidden characteristics of souls can be perceived through this lotus-flower, but whether these perceptions convey the truth depends upon the individual concerned having become entirely free from illusions such as those mentioned above. To this end he must have control over everything that works in upon him from the external world. He must reach the stage where he receives no impressions other than those he is willing to receive. He can achieve this faculty only by developing a powerful inner life; by an effort of will he must allow himself to be affected only by things to which he directs his attention, while warding off all other impressions. Whatever he sees he must see because he *wills* to do so, and what he deliberately ignores must literally be non-existent for him. The more vital and energetic the soul's efforts become, the more successfully will this aim be achieved. The pupil must avoid all thoughtless gazing and listening. Only those things to which he turns eye or ear should exist for him. He must so train himself that he need hear nothing, even amid the greatest turmoil, if he is unwilling to hear; he must make his eyes insensitive to things he does not look at deliberately. He must be shielded as by an inner armour against all unconscious impressions. In this connection the pupil must devote particular care to his life of thought. He singles out a thought and endeavours to carry it further only by such thought as he can relate to it consciously and with complete freedom. He rejects casual notions and does not connect one thought with another until he has carefully examined how the second thought arose. He goes still further. If, for instance, he feels a particular antipathy for something, he combats this feeling and endeavours to establish a *conscious* relation to the thing in question. In this way, fewer and fewer unconscious elements will intrude into his soul. Only by such strict self-discipline can the ten-petalled lotus-flower receive the form that is proper to it. The pupil's inner life must become one of attentiveness and he must learn to keep away everything to which he does not wish or ought not to pay attention.

If this strict self-discipline is accompanied by meditation in keeping with the instructions given in Spiritual Science, the lotus-flower in the region of the pit of the stomach comes to maturity in the right way, and light and colour of a spiritual kind are now added to the form and warmth perceptible to the organs described above. Talents and faculties of souls are thereby revealed; also forces and hidden properties of Nature. The colour-aura of living beings becomes visible; our environment manifests its qualities of soul. In all this the very greatest care is necessary, for here the play of unconscious memories is immeasurably active. If this were not so, many people would possess the inner sense in question here, for it comes almost immediately into evidence when the individual concerned has the impressions transmitted by his outer senses so completely under control that they are now dependent on his attention or inattention. Only as long as the power of the outer senses keeps this soul-organ in subjection, and in a state of dullness, does it remain inactive.

Still greater difficulty attends the development of the six-petalled lotus-flower in the centre of the body, for it can be achieved only as the result of complete mastery of the whole man through consciousness of self, so that body, soul and spirit are in perfect harmony. The functions of the body, the inclinations and passions of the soul, the thoughts and ideas of the spirit, must be tuned to perfect unison. The body must be so ennobled and purified that its organs impel the individual to nothing that is not in the service of the soul and spirit. The soul must not be impelled, through the body, to desires and passions which conflict with pure and noble thinking. But the spirit must not dominate the soul with its laws and moral precepts like a slave-driver; the soul must follow these laws and duties out of its own free inclination. The pupil must not feel duty as a power hovering over him to which he unwillingly submits, but rather as something he does because he loves it. He must develop a free soul standing in equilibrium between sense-existence and spirituality. He must reach the stage where he may safely give himself over to his sense-nature, because this has been so purified that it has lost the power to drag him down to its level. It should no longer be necessary for him to curb his passions, because they will follow a right course of their own accord. As long as self-chastisement is necessary, no one can be a pupil at a certain stage of esoteric development. A virtue which the pupil has to force himself to practise is without value. As long as a desire still remains, it disturbs the training, even although efforts are made not to humour it. Nor does it matter whether this desire proceeds more from the body or more from the soul. For example, if someone avoids taking a certain stimulant in order to purify himself by cutting off an enjoyment, this will help him only if the body suffers no harm from the deprivation. If it does suffer harm, this proves that the body demands the stimulant and that abstinence is valueless. The person may actually have to renounce the ideal he is striving for until more favourable physical conditions—perhaps not until another life—are available. In certain circumstances wise renunciation is a far greater achievement than the struggle for something which under the given conditions is unattainable. Indeed, wise renunciation of this kind contributes more towards development than the opposite course can do.

An individual who has developed the six-petalled lotus-flower is able to enjoy community with beings belonging to the higher worlds, though only if their existence manifests itself in the soul-world. The development of this lotus-flower, however, is not recommended in esoteric training before the pupil has made considerable progress on the path which enables him to raise his *spirit* into a still higher world. This entry into the spirit-world proper must always run parallel with the development of the lotus-flowers, or the pupil will fall into confusion and insecurity. True, he would learn to *see*, but he would lack the capacity to form a correct judgment of what he sees.

Now the development of the six-petalled lotus-flower itself provides a certain security against confusion and instability, for it will not be easy to throw into confusion anyone who has achieved perfect equilibrium between sense-activity (body), passion (soul) and idea (spirit). Yet something more than this security is required when through the development of the six-petalled lotus-flower, beings having life and an independent existence are revealed to the individual concerned—beings belonging to a world utterly different from the world known to his physical senses. The development of the lotus-flowers alone does not ensure for him sufficient security in these higher worlds;

he must have still higher organs at his disposal. The development of these organs will now be described. It will then be possible to speak about the other lotus-flowers and the further organisation of the soul-body.*

The development of the soul-body as described above enables an individual to perceive supersensible phenomena, but anyone who is intent upon finding his bearings in this higher world must not remain stationary at this stage of development. Mere mobility of the lotus-flowers does not suffice. The individual must be in a position to regulate and control independently and with full consciousness the movement of his spiritual organs. Otherwise he would become a plaything of external forces and powers. To avoid this he must acquire the faculty of hearing what is called the 'inner word', and this entails the development not only of the soul-body but also of the etheric body. The latter is the fine, delicate body that is revealed to the clair-voyant as a kind of 'double' of the physical body. It forms as it were an intermediate stage between the physical body and the soul-body.† It is possible for one possessed of clairvoyant faculties consciously to suggest away the

* This expression, though obviously contradictory when taken literally, is used because to clairvoyant sight the impression received spiritually is in keeping with the impression received physically when the physical body is perceived.

† Compare the description with that given in the book *Theosophy* (pp. 26-28, also 142-144, in the 1965 edition).

physical body of a person in front of him. On a higher plane this corresponds to nothing more than an exercise in attentiveness on a lower plane. Just as a man can divert his attention from something in front of him so that it is simply not there for him, the clairvoyant can eliminate a physical body altogether from his field of observation, so that it becomes physically transparent to him. If he applies this faculty to some person standing before him, the so-called etheric body* remains visible to his eyes of soul, as well as the soul-body which is larger than the other two and permeates them both. The etheric body has *approximately* the size and form of the physical body, so that it occupies virtually the same space. It is an extremely fine and delicately organised structure. Its basic colour is different from the seven colours contained in the rainbow. Anyone able to observe it will detect a colour that is actually non-existent for sense-perception and can best be compared to the colour of young peach-blossom. If it is desired to study the etheric body, the soul-body too must be eliminated from observation by an exercise of attentiveness similar to that described above. Otherwise the picture presented by the etheric body will be changed through its permeation by the soul-body.

Now in the human being the components of the etheric

* I would beg the physicists not to take exception to the expression 'etheric body'. The word 'etheric' is used merely to indicate the fineness of the body in question and need not in any way be connected with the hypothetical ether of physics.

body are in continuous movement. Numberless currents pass through it in every direction, and by these currents life is sustained and regulated. Every *living* body has an etheric body—plants and animals too. Even in minerals traces of it can be detected by an acute observer. These currents and movements are, to begin with, entirely independent of man's volition and consciousness, just as the activity of the heart or stomach in the physical body is not dependent upon his conscious will. And this independence remains as long as an individual does not take in hand the development of his supersensible faculties. For at a certain stage, higher development consists precisely in the fact that to the currents and movements of a person's etheric body, which are independent of his consciousness, others consciously produced by himself are added.

When esoteric development has progressed so far that the lotus-flowers begin to stir, the pupil has already achieved a great deal towards stimulating certain quite definite currents and movements in his esoteric body. The object of this development is the formation in the region of the physical heart of a kind of centre, from which currents and movements radiate in the greatest variety of spiritual colours and forms. This centre is not a mere point but a highly complex structure, a wonderful organ. It glows and shimmers spiritually in a myriad colours and exhibits forms of high symmetry, capable of rapid transformation. Other forms and streams of colour radiate from this organ to the other parts of the body and beyond it, permeating and illuminating the whole soul-body. The most important of these currents, however, flow to the lotus-flowers. They permeate each petal and regulate its revolutions; then, streaming out at the tips of the petals, they lose themselves in outer space. The greater the development an individual has achieved, the wider is the environment into which these currents extend.

The twelve-petalled lotus-flower has a particularly close connection with this central organ. The currents flow directly into and through it, proceeding on the one side to the sixteen- and the two-petalled lotus-flowers, and on the other, the lower side, to the eight-, six-, and four-petalled flowers. That is why the very greatest care must be devoted in esoteric training to the development of the twelve-petalled lotus-flower. Any imperfection there would throw the whole formation into disorder. This will indicate the delicate and intimate nature of esoteric training, and the accuracy of procedure needed if everything is to develop as it should. It will also be evident that instruction for the development of supersensible faculties can be given only by one who has himself experienced everything he has to awaken in another and is unquestionably in a position to know whether the instruction he gives is leading to the right results.

If the pupil carries out the instructions given him, he brings into his etheric body currents and movements which are in harmony with the laws and the evolution of the world to which man belongs. Hence these instructions are always a reflection of the great laws of cosmic evolution. They consist of the above-mentioned and similar exercises in meditation and concentration, which, if correctly practised, produce the effects described. The pupil of Spiritual Science must at certain times permeate his soul with the content of the exercises so that he is inwardly filled with it. A simple start is made, designed, above all, to deepen and intensify intelligent, rational thinking. This thinking is thereby made free and independent of all physical sense-impressions and experiences. It is concentrated, as it were, in a single point which is entirely under the person's control. Thereby a provisional centre is created for the currents of the etheric body. This centre is not yet in the region of the heart, but in the head, and to the clairvoyant, it appears as the starting-point of movements. The only esoteric training that can be completely successful is one which first creates this centre. If the centre were formed in the region of the heart from the very beginning, the incipient clairvoyant might certainly have glimpses of the higher worlds, but he would have no true insight into the connection of these higher worlds with our physical world. And this is an unconditional necessity for man at the present stage of evolution. The clairvoyant must not become a fancy-ridden visionary; he *must* keep solid ground under his feet.

The centre in the head, once duly established, is then transferred lower down, to the region of the larynx. This is brought about by further practice of the exercises in concentration. Then the currents of the etheric body radiate from this region and illumine the soul-space around the individual.

Further practice enables the pupil to determine for himself the position of his etheric body. Hitherto this had depended upon forces coming from outside and from the physical body. Through further development the pupil is able to turn his etheric body in any direction. This faculty is produced by currents which move approximately along both hands and are centred in the two-petalled lotus-flower in the region of the eyes. All this is made possible by the radiations from the larynx assuming rounded forms, a number of which flow to the two-petalled lotus-flower and thence move as undulating currents along the hands. As a further development these currents branch out and ramify in the most delicate way, becoming a kind of web which then transforms itself into a membrane (network) round the boundary of the whole etheric body. Previously the etheric body was not closed against the outer world, so that the life-currents from the ocean of universal life streamed freely in and out, but now these currents have to pass through this membrane. Thereafter the individual becomes sensitive to these currents from outside; they become perceptible to him. And now comes the time to give the whole system of currents and movements a centre in the region of the heart. This again is achieved by continuing the practice of concentration and meditation. And at this point, also, the stage is reached when the pupil can hear the 'inner word'. All things now acquire a new significance for him. They become as it were spiritually audible in their inmost nature and speak to him of their essential being. The currents described set him in touch with the inner nature of the world to which he belongs. He begins to participate in the life of his environment and can let it reverberate in the movements of the lotus-flowers.

At this point the spiritual world is entered. If the individual has advanced to this stage, he acquires a new understanding of the utterances of the great Teachers of humanity. The sermons of the Buddha, and the Gospels, for instance, have a new effect upon him. They pervade him with a feeling of beatitude of which he previously had no inkling. For the ring of their words accords with the movements and rhythms he has now developed in himself. He can now have direct *knowledge* that a being such as Buddha and the writers of the Gospels were not giving utterance to their personal revelations but to those which flowed into them from the innermost essence of things.

Here we must draw attention to something that becomes intelligible only in the light of what has been said above. The reason for the many repetitions in the sayings of the Buddha is not rightly understood by people at our present stage of culture. For the esoteric pupil, however, they become something on which he thankfully lets his inner senses rest, for they correspond with certain rhythmic movements in his etheric body. A devotional surrender to the repetitions, in perfect inward calm, creates an inner harmony with these movements, and because the latter reflect particular cosmic rhythms, which also at certain points repeat themselves and revert to their former modes, a person who listens in this way to the wisdom of the Buddha unites himself with the mysteries of the universe.

Spiritual Science speaks of *four* attributes which must be acquired on the so-called probationary path for the attainment of higher knowledge. The *first* is the faculty to discriminate in thought between truth and appearance or semblance, truth and mere opinion. The *second* attribute is the power to value rightly the true and the real, as against the merely apparent. The *third* consists in the practice of the six qualities already described in the preceding pages: control of thoughts, control of actions, perseverance, tolerance, faith and equanimity. The *fourth* attribute is the love of inner freedom.

A mere intellectual grasp of what lies in these attributes is of no use. They must be so deeply integrated into the soul that they become the basis of inner *habits*. Consider, for example, the first attribute: discrimination between truth and semblance. The individual must so train himself that quite as a matter of course he discriminates in everything that confronts him, between the non-essential and the significant. He can succeed in this training only if in his observations of the external world he quietly and patiently repeats the attempt over and over again. In the end he will naturally single out the essential at a glance just as formerly the non-essential satisfied him. 'All things transitory are but a parable'—is a truth which becomes a natural conviction of the soul. And it will be the same with the other three attributes.

Now the delicate etheric body of man is in very fact transformed under the influence of these four habits of the soul. By the first—'discrimination between truth and semblance'—the centre already described is produced in the head, and the centre in the region of the larynx prepared. The actual development of these centres depends on the exercises in concentration referred to above; these exercises are responsible for development, and the four habits bring the centres to fruition. Once the centre in the region of the larynx has been prepared, free control of the etheric body and its envelopment in a network covering, as explained above, are brought about through the right valuing of what is true, as opposed to unreal appearance. If the pupil succeeds in acquiring this faculty of valuing rightly, spiritual realities will gradually become perceptible to him. But he must not think that he has merely to perform actions which appear significant when judged by a mere rational valuation. The most trifling action, every little accomplishment, has some significance in the vast household of the universe and it is only a matter of being *conscious* of this. There must be a right valuation, not an under-valuation, of the everyday affairs of life. The six virtues out of which the third attribute takes shape have already been spoken of. They are connected with the development of the twelve-petalled lotus-flower in the region of the heart and, as already indicated, it is to this centre that the life-currents of the etheric body must be directed. The fourth attribute, the longing for liberation, serves to bring to maturity the etheric organ in the region of the heart. Once this attribute becomes an inner habit, the individual frees himself from everything that is connected *only* with the faculties of his personal nature. He ceases to view things from his own special standpoint, and the limits of his narrow self, which fetter him to this standpoint, disappear. The secrets of the spiritual world reveal themselves to his inner self. This is liberation; for it is those fetters which compel a person to view things and beings according to his personal idiosyncracies. And it is from this personal way of viewing things that the pupil must get free.

It will be clear from the above that the directions given by Spiritual Science work deeply and incisively into the very core of human nature. This applies to the directions concerning the four attributes named above. They are to be found in one form or another in all world-conceptions which take the spirit into account. The precepts given to mankind by the inaugurators of these world-conceptions come not from vague feelings but from the fact that these inaugurators were great Initiates. They knew well how these teachings influence the finer nature of man and desired that their followers should gradually cultivate the development of this finer nature. To live in conformity with these world-conceptions means to work for the attainment of one's own spiritual perfection, and only by so doing can a man truly serve the world. To aim at self-perfection is by no means a matter of self-interest, for an imperfect man is also an imperfect servant of humanity. The more perfect a man is, the better does he serve the whole. 'If the rose adorns herself, she adorns the garden.'

The inaugurators of the important world-conceptions are therefore the great Initiates. What comes from them, streams into the souls of men and so the whole world, together with humanity, makes progress. The Initiates have worked consciously to further this evolutionary process. The content of their teachings can be understood only if it is remembered that these teachings are derived from knowledge of the innermost depths of human nature. The Initiates were *knowers* and out of their knowledge they have shaped the ideals of humanity. But man is able to draw near to these great leaders when he raises himself, through his own development, to their heights.

A completely new life opens out for the individual when the development of his etheric body has begun in the way described above, and through his esoteric training he must receive at the right moment the enlightenment which enables him to find his bearings in this new existence. Through the sixteen-petalled lotus-flower, for instance, he perceives spiritual figures of a higher world. He must now realise how different these forms are, according to whether they originate from this or that object or being. He will notice, first of all, that through his own thoughts and feelings he can exert a strong influence upon certain categories of these figures; on others little or none. The figures belonging to one category will change immediately if, when they appear, the observer has the thought, 'That is beautiful', and then in the course of his contemplation changes the thought to, 'That is useful'. It is characteristic of the forms originating from minerals or from artificial objects that they change under the influence of every thought and feeling directed to them by the observer. This applies in a lesser degree to the forms coming from plants, and less still to those corresponding to animals. These figures, too, are mobile and full of life, but this mobility is due only partially to the influence of the thoughts and feelings of human beings; in other respects it is produced by causes on which man has no influence. But now there appears within this whole world a species of forms which, to begin with, remain almost entirely unaffected by human influence. The esoteric pupil can convince himself that these forms originate neither from minerals nor from artificial objects, nor from plants or animals. In order to be perfectly clear he must study the forms which he knows have been caused by the feelings, impulses and passions of other human beings. But he can discover that these forms, too, are influenced by his own thoughts and feelings, although only to a comparatively slight extent. Within the world of forms there is always a residuum upon which this influence is almost at vanishing point. Indeed, at the beginning of the pupil's development this residuum forms a very considerable part of all that he sees. He can be clear about its nature only by observing *himself*. He then discovers which forms he has himself produced. His own actions, desires, wishes and so forth come to expression in these forms. An impulse that is in him, a desire that he has, an intention that he harbours—all this manifests itself in these forms; indeed his whole character displays itself in this world of forms.

Through his conscious thought-forms and feelings man can exert an influence upon all forms which do not proceed from himself; but he has no influence upon the figures created by his own being in the higher worlds, once he has created them. It follows from what has been said that to higher vision man's inner life of impulses, desires and mental concepts displays itself in *outward* forms, just as is the case with other objects and beings.

To higher knowledge, the inner world becomes part of the outer world. Just as someone in the physical world entirely surrounded by mirrors could observe his physical body on all sides, so too, in a higher world, man's soul-being confronts him as a mirror-image.

At this stage of development the esoteric pupil has reached the point when he overcomes the illusion derived from the enclosure of his personal self. He can now observe the inner content of his personality as outer world, just as hitherto he regarded as outer world everything that affected his senses. In this way he learns by gradual experience to deal with himself as previously he dealt with the beings around him.

If a man were to glimpse these higher worlds without being adequately prepared to understand their nature, the picture of his own soul would confront him like a riddle. His own impulses and passions stand before him there in forms which he feels to be of an animal or—less often—of a human character. True, the animal forms of this world are never quite like those of the physical world, yet there is a remote resemblance. Inexperienced observers will often take them to be identical. Upon entering this world, an entirely new way of forming judgments must be acquired. For, apart from the fact that things actually belonging to man's inner nature appear as outer world, they appear also as the mirror-images of what they really are. When, for instance, a number is perceived, it must be read in reverse: 265 would be, in reality, 562. A sphere is perceived as though from its centre. This view from within must then be correctly translated. Attributes of soul also appear in mirror-images. A wish directed towards some outer object appears as a form moving towards the wisher himself. Passions seated in man's lower nature may assume the forms of animals or similar figures which hurl themselves upon the individual concerned. In reality these passions are struggling outwards; they are looking for satisfaction in the outer world, but this struggle outwards appears in the mirror-image as an attack on the individual who harboured the passion.

If before achieving higher vision the pupil has learnt by calm, objective self-observation to know the essential nature of his own qualities and attributes, then, at the moment when his own inner self confronts him as a mirror-image, he will have courage and strength to conduct himself rightly. Those who through self-examination have not succeeded in acquiring adequate knowledge of their own inner nature will not recognise *themselves* in their own mirror-image and will take it to be an extraneous reality. Or they become alarmed at the sight, and, finding it unendurable, persuade themselves that the whole thing is nothing but a product of fantasy which can lead nowhere. In both cases the individual involved, through having attained a certain stage of development prematurely, would disastrously obstruct his own progress.

It is essential that the pupil should have spiritual perception of his own soul before advancing to a higher stage. For he has in his own self the entity of soul and spirit which he is most capable of judging. If he has acquired a thorough knowledge of his own personality in the physical world, when the *image* of his personality first confronts him in the higher world, he is able to compare the one with the other. He can relate the higher phenomenon to something already known to him and in this way have a firm foundation. On the other hand, however many other spiritual beings were to appear before him, he would be quite unable to discern their individual qualities and nature and would soon feel the ground slipping from under his feet. Hence it cannot be too often emphasised that the only safe access to the higher world is gained by a path leading through genuine knowledge and assessment of one's own being.

Hence it is spiritual pictures that a man first encounters on his path to the higher world; and the reality which corresponds to these pictures lies actually *within himself*. Accordingly he must be mature enough not to demand hard-and-fast realities at this initial stage, but to regard these pictures as appropriate. But within this world of pictures he will soon learn something quite new. His *lower self* is before him as a mirror-image only; but within this image there appears the true reality of the *higher Self*. The form of the spiritual Ego becomes visible out of the picture of the lower personality. Threads are then spun from the spiritual Ego to other, higher spiritual realities.

And now the time has come to make use of the two-petalled lotus-flower in the region of the eyes. When it moves, the individual finds it possible to establish a connection between his higher Ego and lofty spiritual Beings. The currents from this lotus-flower stream to higher realities in such a way that the individual in question is fully conscious of the movements. Just as the light makes physical objects visible to the eyes, so do these currents make visible the spiritual Beings of higher worlds.

Through deep contemplation of the fundamental truths contained in the concepts and ideas of Spiritual Science, the pupil learns to set in motion and to direct the currents proceeding from the lotus-flower between the eyes.

It is at this stage of development especially that training in sound judgment and clear, logical thinking proves its value. The higher Self, which has hitherto slumbered unconsciously in an embryonic state, is now born into conscious existence. This is not a figurative event, but a veritable birth in the spiritual world, and if the higher Self having now been born, is to be capable of life, it must enter that world with all the necessary organs and aptitudes. Just as nature must see to it that a child is born into the world with well-formed ears and eyes, so must the laws of man's own development ensure that his higher Self comes into existence with the necessary faculties. And these laws, which govern the development of the higher organs of the spirit, are none other than the laws of healthy reason and morality belonging to the physical world. The spiritual man matures in the physical self as a child in the mother's womb. The health of the child depends upon the normal working of natural laws in the mother's womb. The health of the spiritual man is similarly conditioned by the laws of ordinary intelligence and reason working in physical life. No one can give birth to a healthy higher Self who does not live and think in a healthy way in the physical world. A natural and rational way of living are the basis of all true spiritual development. Just as the child in the mother's womb already lives in accordance with the forces of nature of which it becomes aware after birth through its organs of sense, so does the higher Self live in accordance with the laws of the spiritual world, even during physical existence.

And just as the child, out of a dim instinct, acquires forces requisite for life, so can man acquire the powers of the spiritual world before his higher Self is born. Indeed, he *must* do so if the higher Self is to come into the world as a fully developed being. It would not be right for anyone to say: 'I cannot accept the teachings of Spiritual Science before I am myself a seer,' for without inner application to the findings of Spiritual Science there is no chance whatever of acquiring genuine higher knowledge. He would then be in the same situation as a child in the womb who refused to make use of the forces coming to it through the mother and wished to wait until it could create them itself. Just as the embryonic child with its incipient feeling for life accepts as right what is offered to it, so can a man who is not yet a seer accept the truth of the teachings of Spiritual Science. Insight into these teachings, based on a feeling for truth and clear, sound, comprehensive judgment, is possible even before spiritual things are actually seen. One must study the testimonies of mystical knowledge to begin with, and through this study prepare oneself for vision. A person who has vision without such preparation would be like a child born with eyes and ears but without a brain. The world of sounds and colours would be spread out before him, but he would be unable to make anything of it.

A person who has reached the stage of esoteric discipleship we have just described finds that what had previously appealed to his sense of truth, intellect and reason becomes a personal experience. He now has direct knowledge of his higher Self. He learns to know how his higher Self is connected with lofty spiritual Beings and forms a unity with them. He perceives how the lower self stems from a higher world and it is revealed to him that his higher nature outlasts the lower. He can now himself distinguish the perishable within him from the imperishable. This means that through his own perception he learns to understand the teaching of the incorporation (incarnation) of the higher Self in a lower self. It is now clear to him that he is involved in a higher, spiritual complex of circumstances, and that his qualities and destiny are the outcome of this. He learns to recognise the *law of his life*, his Karma. He realises that his lower self, in his present existence, is only one of the forms which his higher Self can adopt. He discerns the possibility of working from his higher Self upon his lower self, so that he may come nearer and nearer to the ideal. He can now also discern the great differences between human beings in respect of their degree of development. He becomes aware that there are men of higher rank than his own who have already reached the stages which still lie ahead of him, and he realises that the teachings and deeds of such men proceed from the inspirations coming from a higher world. He owes this knowledge to his own first glimpse into this higher world. The persons called the 'great Initiates of humanity' will now begin to be realities for him.

These, then, are the gifts which the esoteric pupil owes to his development at this stage: insight into the higher

Self, into the teaching of the incarnation of this higher Self into a lower, into the law by which life in the physical world is regulated according to spiritual relationships—that is, the law of Karma—and finally, insight into the existence of the great Initiates.

It is therefore also said of a pupil who has reached this stage that all *doubt* has vanished from him. His former faith, based on reason and sound thinking, is now replaced by knowledge and insight which nothing can shatter.

In their ceremonies, sacraments and rites the religions have presented outwardly visible pictures of higher spiritual processes and beings. Only those who have not yet penetrated to the depths of the great religions can fail to recognise this. Anyone who has actual vision of spiritual reality will also understand the great significance of those outwardly visible acts. Religious worship itself then becomes for him an image of his communion with the higher, spiritual world.

We see how by reaching this stage the pupil has veritably become a new being. He can now gradually mature to the stage where by means of the currents of his etheric body he can direct and control the higher life-element, and thereby achieve a high measure of freedom from his physical body.

CHANGES IN DREAM LIFE

An intimation that the pupil has reached or will soon reach the stage of development described in the preceding chapter will be the change which takes place in his dream life. His dreams, hitherto confused and haphazard, now begin to assume a more regular character. Their pictures begin to arrange themselves in an orderly way, like the thoughts and ideas of daily life. The pupil can discern in them law, cause and effect. The content of the dreams also changes. Whereas previously he discerned only reminiscences of everyday life and transformed impressions of his surroundings or of his own physical condition, there now appear before him pictures of a world previously unknown to him. At first the *general character* of his dream life remains unchanged, in so far as the dream is distinguished from waking mental activity by the fact that it presents in *symbol* what it wants to express. No attentive observer of dream life can fail to detect this characteristic. For instance, you may dream that you have caught some horrible creature and feel an unpleasant sensation in your hand. On waking you discover that you are squeezing a corner of the bedspread. The perception does not, therefore, express itself undisguised, but through this symbolical image. You may dream that you are running away from some pursuer and are stricken with fear. On waking, you find that during sleep you have been suffering from palpitations of the heart. Disquieting dreams can also be traced to indigestible food. Occurrences in the immediate vicinity may also reflect themselves symbolically in dreams. The striking of a clock may evoke the picture of a troop of soldiers marching by to the beat of drums. A falling chair may give rise to a whole drama in which the sound of the fall is reproduced in the dream as the report of a gun, and so forth. The more regulated dreams of the pupil whose etheric body has begun to develop retain this symbolical mode of expression, but they will no longer reflect merely facts connected with the physical body or the physical environment. As the dreams due to these factors become regulated, they are mingled with pictures expressing things and events of another world.

These are the first experiences lying beyond the range of waking consciousness. Yet no genuine mystic will ever make his experiences in dreams the basis of any authoritative account of a higher world. Such dreams must be considered merely as providing the first hint of higher development. Very soon, and as a further result, the pupil's dreams will no longer remain beyond the reach of intellectual guidance, but on the contrary will be ordered and comprehended, like the ideas and perceptions of waking consciousness. The difference between dream consciousness and waking consciousness becomes constantly less. The dreamer remains awake in the fullest sense of the word

161

during his dream life; that is to say he feels himself to be master and controller of his mental pictures.

During his dreams the individual is actually in a world different from that of his physical senses; but with undeveloped spiritual organs he can form only the confused conceptions described above. It is present for him only as far as the world of the senses could be for a being having no more than the most rudimentary eyes. That is why he can see nothing in this world except reflections of everyday life. The latter are perceptible to him because his own soul paints its daily experiences in pictorial form into the substance of which that other world consists. It must be clearly understood that in addition to a man's ordinary conscious waking life, he leads a second, unconscious life in that other world. He engraves into it all his thoughts and perceptions. These tracings become visible only when the lotus-flowers are developed.

Now in every human being there are certain scanty beginnings of these lotus-flowers. He can perceive nothing with them during waking consciousness because the impressions made upon them are very faint. For a similar reason he cannot see the stars during the daytime: their visibility is extinguished by the powerful light of the sun. Thus, too, the faint impressions from the spiritual world cannot make themselves felt in face of the powerful impressions received through the physical senses.

When the gates of the senses are closed during sleep, these other impressions begin to emerge confusedly, and the dreamer becomes aware of experiences undergone in another world. But, as already explained, these experiences consist, at first, merely of pictures engraved in the spiritual world by the mental activity attached to the physical senses. Developed lotus-flowers alone make it possible for manifestations not derived from the physical world to be imprinted in the same way. And then the etheric body, when developed, brings full knowledge concerning these engraved impressions that are derived from other worlds. This is the beginning of life and activity in a new world and at this point esoteric training must set the pupil a twofold task. To begin with he must learn to take stock of everything he observes in his dreams, exactly as though he were awake. Then, if successful in this, he is led to make the same observations during ordinary waking consciousness. He will so train his receptivity for these spiritual impressions that they need no longer vanish in the face of the physical impressions, but will always be at hand for him and reach him in addition to the physical ones.

When the pupil has acquired this faculty there arises before his spiritual eyes something of the picture described in the preceding chapter, and he can henceforth discern what is present in the spiritual world as the cause of the physical world. Above all he can recognise his own higher Self in this world. His next task is to grow, as it were, into this higher Self, actually to regard it as his own true being and to conduct himself accordingly. He realises ever more clearly that his physical body and what he had hitherto called his 'I' are merely instruments of the higher Self. He adopts an attitude towards his lower self such as a person limited to the world of the senses adopts towards some instrument or vehicle that serves him. Nobody includes as part of himself the vehicle in which he is travelling, even though he says: 'I am travelling.' When an inwardly developed person says: 'I go through the door,' his actual concept is: 'I carry my body through the door.' This must become a natural habit with him, so that he never for a moment loses his firm footing in the physical world or feels estranged from it. If the pupil is to avoid becoming a fancy-ridden visionary he must not impoverish his life through his higher consciousness but on the contrary enrich it, as a person enriches his life by using the railway and not his legs to go for a long journey.

When the pupil has thus raised himself to a life in the higher 'I'—or rather during his acquisition of the higher consciousness—he will learn how to stir to life the force of spiritual perception in the organ lying in the region of the heart, and control it through the currents described in the previous chapter. This perceptive force is an element of higher substantiality which proceeds from the organ in question and flows with radiant beauty through the moving lotus-flowers and the other channels of the developed etheric body. Thence it radiates outwards into the surrounding spiritual world, rendering it spiritually visible, just as the sunlight falling upon the objects of the physical world renders them visible.

How this perceptive force in the heart-organ is produced can be understood only gradually in the course of actual development.

It is only when this means of perception can be sent through the etheric body and into the outer world, to illumine it, that the objects and beings of the spiritual world can be clearly perceived. Thus it will be seen that full consciousness of an object in the spiritual world is possible only when man himself casts upon it this spiritual light. Now the 'I' which creates this organ of perception does not dwell within, but outside, the physical body, as already shown. The heart-organ is only the place where the individual kindles from without this source of spiritual light. Were the light kindled elsewhere, the spiritual perceptions produced by it would have no connection with the physical world. But all higher spiritual realities must be related to the physical world and man himself must act as a channel for them to flow into it. It is precisely through the heart-organ that the higher 'I' makes the physical self its instrument.

The feeling which a developed individual has for the things of the spiritual world differs from that of an ordinary man for the physical world. The latter feels himself to be at a particular place in the world of sense and the objects perceived to be 'outside' him. The spiritually developed individual, on the other hand, feels himself to be united with, and as though within, the spiritual objects he perceives. He actually wanders from place to place in spiritual space, and is therefore called the 'wanderer' in the language of occult science. To begin with, he is nowhere at home. Should he remain a mere wanderer, he would be unable to define clearly any object in spiritual space. Just as objects and places in physical space are determined from a certain point of departure, this too must be so in the other world. The pupil must seek out some place which he has thoroughly explored and take possession of it spiritually. In this place he must establish a spiritual home for himself and relate everything else to it. In physical life, too, a person sees everything in terms of the mental pictures associated with his physical home. A native of Berlin will involuntarily describe London differently from the way in which a Parisian will describe it. Only there is a difference between the spiritual and the physical home. We are born into the latter without our participation and during our youth absorb instinctively a number of ideas by which everything is henceforth involuntarily coloured. The pupil, however, has himself founded his spiritual home, in full consciousness. His judgment, therefore, based on this spiritual home, is formed in full, unhampered freedom. This founding of a spiritual home is called in the language of occult science, 'building a hut'.

Spiritual vision at this stage extends to the counterparts of the physical world, as far as these exist in the so-called astral world. In this world there is found everything which, in its nature, is similar to human instincts, feelings, desires and passions. For forces related to these human characteristics are associated with all physical objects. A crystal, for instance, is cast into its form by forces which, seen from a higher vantage-point, appear as an impulse which is active also in human beings. Similar forces drive the sap through the vessels of the plant, cause the blossoms to unfold and the seed vessels to burst. To developed spiritual organs of perception, all these forces acquire form and colour, just as the objects of the physical world have form and colour for physical eyes. At this stage in his development, the pupil sees not only the crystal and the plant, but also their characteristic spiritual forces. Animal and human impulses are perceptible to him not only through the physical manifestations in their bearers, but directly as objects, just as he sees tables and chairs in the physical world. The whole range of instinct, impulse, desire and passion, whether of an animal or of a human being, becomes an astral cloud or aura in which the being is enveloped.

Furthermore, the clairvoyant can at this stage perceive things which are almost entirely withheld from the senses. He can, for instance, discern the astral difference between a room mainly occupied by people with base intentions or one in which those with good purposes are present. Not only the physical but also the spiritual atmosphere of a hospital differs from that of a dance-hall. A commercial town has a different astral atmosphere from that of a university town. At the initial stages of clairvoyance, this perceptive faculty is only weakly developed; its relation to the objects in question is similar to the relation of dream consciousness to waking consciousness in everyday life; in time, however, it will be fully awakened at this stage also.

The highest achievement of a clairvoyant who has attained the degree of vision described above is when the astral counterparts of animal and human impulses and passions are revealed to him. A loving action is accompanied by a different astral picture from one inspired by hatred. Unbridled desire gives rise to an ugly astral counterpart, while a feeling evoked by a high ideal gives rise to one of beauty. These astral counterparts are only faintly perceptible during the physical life of an individual, for their strength is diminished by conditions of existence in the physical world. A desire for an object produces a corresponding image which appears in the astral world as the desire itself. If, however, the object is attained and the desire satisfied, or if the possibility of satisfaction is there, the corresponding image will be only faint. It attains its full strength only after the death of the individual, when the soul, in accordance with its nature, still cherishes such a desire but can no longer satisfy it because both the object and the physical organ are lacking. The gourmand, for example, will retain after death the desire to please his palate; but there is no possibility of satisfying his desire because he no longer has a palate. The result is that the desire produces an especially powerful counterpart, by which the soul is tormented. These experiences evoked after death by the images of the lower soul-nature are known as the experiences in the soul-world, especially in the region of desires. They do not vanish until the soul has cleansed itself of all appetites concerned with the physical world. Then only does the soul rise to the higher region, to the world of spirit. Even though these images are faint during life in the physical world, they are none the less present, following the individual as his world of desire, as a comet is followed by its tail. They can be seen by a clairvoyant at the corresponding stage of development.

Such and similar experiences fill the life of the pupil during the period described above. Higher spiritual experiences are beyond his reach at this stage of development. He must climb on to a still higher level.

CONTINUITY OF CONSCIOUSNESS

The life of man runs its course in three alternating states—waking, dreaming sleep, dreamless sleep. How the higher knowledge of spiritual worlds is achieved can be readily understood if an idea is formed of the changes in these three states which must take place in an individual seeking higher knowledge. Before training has been undertaken, man's consciousness is continually interrupted by the periods of sleep. During these periods the soul knows nothing either of the outer world or of itself. It is only at certain times that dreams arise from the ocean of unconsciousness, dreams related to happenings in the outer world or to conditions in the physical body itself. At first, dreams are regarded merely as a particular manifestation of sleep-life, and so only two states are usually spoken of—sleeping and waking. For Spiritual Science, however, dreams have a special significance, apart from the other two conditions. In the previous chapter a description was given of the change occurring in the dream-life of an individual undertaking the ascent to higher knowledge. His dreams lose their meaningless, disorderly and disjointed character and become more and more coherent and orderly. With continued development, not only does this new world that has been born out of the dream-world come to be in no way inferior to outer, physical reality in respect of inner truth, but the facts it reveals represent a higher reality in the fullest sense of the word.

Mysteries and riddles lie hidden everywhere in the phenomenal world. In the latter, the *effects* of certain higher facts are seen, but no one whose perception is confined to his senses can penetrate to the *causes*. These causes are partially revealed to the pupil in the condition that develops out of dream-life—a condition, however, which by no means remains stationary. Yet he must not regard these revelations as actual knowledge, so long as the same things do not also reveal themselves during ordinary waking life. In time he learns to carry over into waking consciousness the condition he first created for himself out of dream-life. Then something quite new enriches the world of his senses. Just as a person born blind and successfully operated upon will find the surrounding objects enriched by everything that the eyes perceive, so too will anyone who has become clairvoyant in the above manner perceive new qualities, new things, new beings and so forth, in the world around him. He now need no longer wait for dreams in order to live in another world, for at any suitable moment he can transfer himself into the above condition for the purpose of higher perception. This condition is then comparable to the perception of things with active senses as opposed to inactive senses. It can truly be said that the pupil opens the eyes of his soul and beholds things which must remain concealed from the bodily senses.

Now this condition is only transitional to still higher

stages of knowledge. If the pupil continues the exercises connected with his training, he will find in due time that the radical change described above is not confined to his dream-life, but that this transformation extends also to what was previously a condition of deep, dreamless sleep. Isolated conscious experiences begin to interrupt the complete insensibility of this deep sleep. Perceptions previously unknown to him emerge from the pervading darkness of sleep. It is not easy to describe these perceptions, for our language has been created for the physical world alone and only approximate terms can be found for what simply does not belong to that world. Yet such terms must be used to describe the higher worlds and this is possible only by the free use of a simile; but since everything in the world is inter-related, this can be done. The things and beings of the higher worlds are related to those of the physical world closely enough to ensure that with a measure of good-will some conception of these higher worlds can be formed, even though words suitable for the physical world have to be used. Only it must always be kept in mind that much in these descriptions of supersensible worlds is bound to be in the nature of simile and symbol. In esoteric training, therefore, the words of ordinary language are used only to a limited extent; for the rest, the pupil learns another symbolical language as a natural outcome of his ascent to higher worlds. Knowledge of this language must be acquired during training, but that is no reason why something concerning the higher worlds should not be learned even from ordinary descriptions such as those given here.

An idea of the experiences which emerge from the unconsciousness of deep sleep can best be conveyed if they are compared to a kind of *hearing*. We can speak of audible tones and words. While the experiences during dreaming sleep may fitly be designated as a kind of *seeing*, by comparison with the perceptions of the senses, the facts observed during deep sleep may be compared to auditory impressions. (It should be remarked in passing that in the spiritual worlds, too, the faculty of *seeing* or *beholding* is the higher. In that world, too, colours are at a higher level than sounds and words. But the pupil's first perceptions in this world do not include these higher colours, but only the lower tones. It is only because the human being, in line with his general development, is more qualified for the world revealed in dreaming sleep that straightway he perceives colours there. He is less qualified for the higher world that reveals itself to him in deep sleep; therefore this world is revealed to him at first in tones and words; later on he can rise also to the level of colours and forms.)

Now when these experiences during deep sleep first come to the notice of the pupil, he must proceed to make them as clear and vivid as possible. To begin with this is very difficult, for awareness of these experiences is at first extremely faint. The pupil knows on waking that he has had an experience, but is completely vague as to its nature. The most important thing during this initial stage is to remain quiet and composed and not for a moment to lapse into any unrest or impatience. These responses are always detrimental; they can never accelerate development, but only delay it. The pupil must cultivate quiet receptivity for whatever is vouchsafed to him; all violent methods must be avoided. Should he at any time cease to be aware of experiences during sleep, he must wait patiently until this is possible again. This moment will assuredly arrive. And this perceptive faculty, if awaited with patience and composure, remains a secure possession; but if once made to manifest by forcible methods, it can be completely lost for a long time.

Once the perceptive faculty is acquired and the experiences during sleep are present to the pupil's consciousness in complete lucidity and clarity, he must direct his attention to the following. These experiences are of two kinds, clearly distinguishable. The first kind will be totally foreign to anything he has ever known. They may be a source of joy and inner nourishment, but they should be left to themselves for the time being. They are the first harbingers of the higher spiritual world in which the pupil will only later find his bearings. In the second kind of experiences the attentive observer will discover a certain relationship with the everyday world in which he lives. The things he reflects about during life, what he would like to understand in his environment but cannot grasp with the ordinary intellect—these are the things concerning which the experiences during sleep give him enlightenment. During everyday life man reflects about his environment; his mind tries to conceive and understand the connections between things; he tries to grasp in ideas and concepts what his senses perceive. It is to these ideas and concepts that the experiences during sleep refer. Obscure, shadowy concepts become resonant and living, in a way comparable only to the tones and words of the world of the senses. More and more it seems to the pupil as though the solution of the riddles over which he ponders is whispered to him in the tones and words from a higher world. And he is then able to connect with ordinary life whatever comes to him from a higher world. What was formerly accessible only to his thought, now becomes actual experience, as living and real as any experience in the world of sense can be. The things and beings of the world of sense are by no means only what they appear to be to physical perception. They are the expression and effluence of a spiritual world. The spiritual world hitherto concealed from the pupil now resounds for him out of his whole environment.

It is easy to see that this higher perceptive faculty can prove a blessing only if the soul-senses that have opened are in perfect order, just as the ordinary senses can be used for accurate observation of the world only if they are in a well-regulated condition. Now the pupil himself forms these higher senses through the exercises indicated in his training. They include concentration, in which the attention is directed to certain definite ideas and concepts connected with the secrets of the universe; and meditation, which is a complete submersion in these concepts in the prescribed way. Through concentration and meditation the pupil works upon his soul and develops in it the soul-organs of perception. While thus applying himself to the task of concentration and meditation, his soul grows within his body just as the embryo grows in the body of the mother. And when the experiences during sleep begin, as described, the moment of birth is approaching for the liberated soul which has literally become a new being, developed by the individual within himself from seed to fruit. The efforts required for concentration and meditation must therefore be accurately and carefully maintained, for they are indeed the laws governing the germination and fruition of the higher being of soul. At its birth, this being must be a harmonious, well-formed organism. But if some part of the directions is carried out wrongly, no living being will come into existence in the spiritual realm, but a being incapable of life.

Why this higher soul-being should be born during deep sleep can be readily understood for if this delicate organism were to appear during physical, everyday life, it could not hold its own against the harsh and strenuous processes of this existence. Its activity, pitted against that of the body, would be of no account. During sleep, however, when the body is at rest in so far as its activity is dependent on *sense-perception*, then the activity of the higher soul, at first so delicate and inconspicuous, can come into evidence. Here again the pupil must bear in mind that these experiences during sleep must not be regarded as fully valid knowledge as long as he is not able to carry over his awakened higher soul into waking consciousness as well. The acquisition of this faculty will enable him to perceive the spiritual world in its own character among and between the experiences of the day; the hidden secrets of his environment will be conveyed to his soul as tones and words.

At this stage of development the pupil must realise that he is dealing with separate, more or less unconnected spiritual experiences. He should therefore beware of constructing out of them a complete whole or even a connected system of knowledge. All kinds of fantastic ideas and conceptions would then be mixed into the soul-world, and a realm might easily be fabricated which had nothing at all to do with the real spiritual world. The pupil must continually practise the strictest self-control. His right course is to strive for an ever clearer conception of the real experiences and to await the spontaneous emergence of new experiences which will link up of their own accord with those already present. By virtue of the power of the spiritual world into which he has now found his way, and through continued application to the prescribed exercises, the pupil experiences an ever-increasing extension and expansion of consciousness during deep sleep. More and more experiences emerge from unconsciousness and the intervals of insensibility become constantly shorter. These experiences increasingly link themselves together of their own accord, without this true union being disturbed by all manner of combinations and conclusions which in any case would originate only in an intellect accustomed to the physical world. But the less the habits of thought acquired in the physical world are allowed to play into these higher experiences, the better it is.

By thus conducting himself, the pupil approaches ever nearer to the attainment of that stage on the path to higher knowledge when the unconsciousness of sleep is transformed into full consciousness. While his body rests, he lives in a world as real as that of waking life. Needless to say, the reality encountered during sleep is different from that of the physical environment in which the body lives. The pupil learns—indeed he must learn if he is to retain a firm footing in the physical world and not become a visionary—to relate the higher experiences of sleep to the physical environment. At first, however, the world experienced during sleep is a completely new revelation. This important stage of development, when consciousness is retained during sleep, is known in Spiritual Science as the continuity of consciousness.*

A man who has reached this stage of development does not cease to have experiences during times when the physical body is at rest and the soul is receiving no impressions through the instrumentality of the senses.

* The condition indicated here is for a certain stage of development a kind of 'ideal', attainable at the end of a long path. What the pupil learns to know to begin with are these two states of the life of soul: consciousness in a state where previously only chaotic dreams were possible, and consciousness in a state previously given over to unconscious, dreamless sleep.

THE DIVISION OF THE PERSONALITY
DURING SPIRITUAL TRAINING

During sleep no communications from the physical sense-organs, no perceptions of the ordinary outer world, find their way to the human soul. In a certain respect the soul is *outside* that part of the human being—of the so-called physical body—which in waking life is the medium for sense-perceptions and for thinking. The soul is then connected only with the finer bodies (etheric body and astral body) which evade observation by the physical senses. But the activity of these finer bodies does not cease during sleep. Just as the physical body is connected with the objects and beings of the physical world, affecting them and being affected by them, so does the soul live in a higher world; and this life of the soul continues during sleep. The soul is fully active during sleep, but a man can know nothing of this, his own activity, as long as he has no spiritual organs of perception through which he can observe what is going on around him and see what he himself is doing during sleep as easily as he can observe his daily physical environment with his ordinary senses. The preceding chapters have shown how esoteric training consists in the development of these organs of spiritual perception.

Now if as a result of esoteric training the pupil's life

during sleep is transformed in the manner described in the previous chapter, he will be able in that condition to follow consciously everything going on around him. He can, at will, find his bearings in his environment just as he could, when awake, with his ordinary senses. It should here be noted, however, that spiritual perception of the ordinary physical environment calls for a higher degree of clairvoyance, as was indicated in the last chapter. In the initial stages of his development, the pupil perceives only things belonging to another world, without being able to discern their connection with the objects of his daily physical environment.

These characteristic examples of life during sleep or in dreams illustrate what is taking place continually in the human being. The soul lives in uninterrupted activity in the higher worlds, gathering from them the impulse to work upon the physical body. But man is *unconscious* of this higher life; the esoteric pupil makes himself conscious of it and thereby his whole life is transformed. As long as the soul is without seership in the higher sense, it is guided by lofty cosmic Beings. And just as the life of a person born blind is transformed through a successful operation from its previous state of dependence upon a guide, so too the life of a person is transformed through esoteric training. He outgrows leadership and must henceforward undertake to be his own guide. As soon as this happens he is, of course, liable to errors totally unknown to ordinary consciousness. He acts now from a world from which higher Powers formerly influenced him, unconsciously to himself. These higher Powers are regulated by the universal cosmic harmony. The pupil emerges from this cosmic harmony and must now himself accomplish things that were previously accomplished for him without his co-operation.

It is for this reason that writings dealing with these matters have much to say about the dangers connected with the ascent into higher worlds. The descriptions sometimes given of these dangers may well make timid souls shudder at the prospect of this higher life. Yet the fact is that dangers arise only when the necessary precautions are neglected. If all the measures advised by true esoteric training are adopted, the ascent will indeed proceed through experiences surpassing in power and magnitude everything that the boldest flights of sense-bound fancy can picture; but there can be no question of injury to health and life. The pupil meets with gruesome powers, threatening life at every turn and from every side. It will even be possible for him to make use of certain forces and beings hidden from sensory perception, and the temptation is great to control these forces for the furtherance of personal and impermissible interests, or to employ them wrongly because of deficient knowledge of the higher worlds. Some of these particularly important experiences (for example, the meeting with the Guardian of the Threshold) will be described in the following chapters. But we must realise that the hostile powers are present even when we know nothing of them. It is true that in this case their relation to man is determined by higher Powers, and that this relation alters when the individual consciously enters this world, hitherto concealed from him. But at the same time his own existence is enhanced and the sphere of his life enriched by a great field of experience. Real danger can arise only if through impatience or arrogance the pupil prematurely assumes a certain independence in his attitude towards the experiences of the higher world, or if he cannot wait to gain sufficient insight into super-sensible laws. In this sphere, modesty and humility are far less empty words than they are in ordinary life. If the pupil possesses these qualities in the best sense, he may be certain that his ascent to the higher life will be achieved without danger to all that is implied by health and life.

Above all, no disharmony must arise between the higher experiences and the events and demands of everyday life. Man's task must be sought on this Earth, and anyone desiring to shirk these tasks and to escape into another world may be certain that he will not reach his goal. But what the senses perceive is only part of the world. The beings who express themselves in the facts of the phenomenal world live in the spiritual. Man must participate in the spirit in order to be able to carry its revelations into the world of the senses. He transforms the Earth by implanting in it what he has discovered in the spiritual world. Therein lies his task. But because the physical Earth is dependent upon the spiritual world, and because man can work upon the

Earth in a true sense only if he is a participator in those worlds where the creative forces lie concealed—for these reasons he should have the will to ascend to the higher worlds. No one who approaches esoteric training with these feelings, and is resolved not to deviate for a moment from the prescribed directives, will have the slightest danger to fear. No one should allow the prospect of these dangers to keep him from esoteric training; he should rather take it as a strong challenge to acquire those faculties which the true esoteric pupil must possess.

After these preliminaries, which should certainly dispel all forebodings, a description of some of the so-called 'dangers' will now be given. It is true that great changes take place in the pupil's finer bodies. These changes are connected with certain processes in the development of the three fundamental forces of the soul: *willing, feeling* and *thinking*. Before esoteric training, these forces are connected in a way ordained by higher, cosmic laws. Man's willing, feeling and thinking are not arbitrary. When a particular idea arises in the mind, a certain feeling is associated with it in accordance with natural laws; or it is followed by a resolution of the will, in equally natural sequence. We go into a room, find it stuffy, and open the windows. We hear our name called, and we follow the call. We are questioned, and we answer. We become aware of an evil-smelling object and experience a feeling of disgust. These are simple examples of connections between thinking, feeling and willing. When we survey human life we find that everything is built on such connections. Indeed a person's life is said to be 'normal' only when such a connection between thinking, feeling and willing, founded on the laws of human nature, can be observed. It would be considered contrary to these laws if the sight of an evil-smelling object gave a person pleasure, or if, on being questioned, he did not answer. The success to be expected from a right kind of upbringing or a suitable education is based on the assumption that a connection between thinking, feeling and willing, in conformity with human nature, can be established in the child. Certain ideas are conveyed to him on the assumption that later on they will be connected in an orderly way with his feelings and his resolves of will. All this arises from the fact that in the finer soul-vehicles of man the central points of the three forces—thinking, feeling and willing—are connected in a regular way. This connection in the finer soul-organism has its counterpart in the coarser physical body. Here, too, the organs of will are connected in an orderly way with those of thinking and feeling. A definite thought evokes a feeling or an activity of will.

In the course of higher development, the threads interconnecting the three fundamental forces are severed. At first this severance occurs only within the finer soul-organism, but at a still higher stage the separation extends to the physical body as well. (It is a fact that in higher spiritual development the brain actually divides into three separate members. This separation, admittedly, is not physically perceptible in the ordinary way, nor can it be demonstrated by the most delicate instruments. But it occurs, and the clairvoyant has means of observing it. The brain of the higher clairvoyant divides into three independently active entities: the thinking-brain, the feeling-brain and the willing-brain.)

Thus the organs of thinking, feeling and willing become individualised and free of each other. Their connection is no longer maintained by laws inherent in themselves but must be cared for by the awakened higher consciousness of the individual. The change noticed by the pupil in himself is that no connection ensues between an idea and a feeling or a will-impulse unless he himself creates one. No impulse leads him from a thought to an action unless he himself freely gives effect to this impulse. Henceforth, he can confront without any feeling a fact which, before his training, would have filled him with ardent love or bitter hatred; he can remain impassive towards a thought which would formerly have spurred him on to action of its own accord. And by efforts of will he can perform actions for which not the slightest cause can be detected by anyone who has not undergone esoteric training. The pupil's great achievement is the attainment of complete mastery over the interconnected activity of the three soul-forces; but at the same time the responsibility for this activity is placed entirely in his own hands.

It is only through this transformation of his being that the pupil can enter into conscious relationship with certain supersensible forces and beings. For his own soul-forces are related to certain fundamental forces of the world. The force inherent in the will, for example, can work upon specific things and beings of the higher worlds, and can also lead to perception of them; but it can do so only when it has become free from its connection with thinking and feeling within the soul. As soon as this connection ceases, the activity of the will manifests outwardly. The same applies to the forces of thinking and feeling. If someone sends a feeling of hatred towards me, this is visible to the clairvoyant as a fine, luminous cloud of a particular colour. And a clairvoyant can ward off this feeling of hatred, just as a person using ordinary senses wards off a physical blow that is aimed at him. In the supersensible world, hatred becomes a visible phenomenon. But the clairvoyant can perceive it only in so far as he is able to project outwards the force inherent in his feeling, just as an ordinary man directs outwards the receptive faculty of his eyes. And what is said of hatred applies to far more important facts of the phenomenal world. The pupil can enter into conscious relationship with them through the liberation of the fundamental forces of his soul.

When this separation of the forces of thinking, feeling and willing come about, the possibility of a threefold aberration on the path of development arises for anyone who neglects the injunctions given by esoteric science. This may occur if the connecting threads are severed before the higher consciousness, with the knowledge belonging to it, is sufficiently advanced to be able to hold the reins whereby free and harmonious cooperation between the separate forces can be established. For as a rule the three fundamental soul-forces are not equally advanced in their development at a given period of life. In one person, thinking is ahead of feeling and willing; in a second, a different soul-force has the upper hand over the others. As long as the connection between the soul-forces is maintained by higher cosmic laws, no injurious irregularity in a higher sense can ensue through the predominance of one force or another. Predominating will, for instance, is prevented by the compensating influence of thinking and feeling from lapsing into special excesses. When, however, a person of predominating will embarks upon esoteric training, feeling and thinking cease to exert their normal influence on the will, as it strives towards fantastic achievements. If, then, such a person is not sufficiently advanced to have complete control over the higher consciousness and so to restore harmony himself, the will pursues its own unbridled way, continually overpowering its possessor. Feeling and thinking lapse into complete impotence; the man is scourged by his overmastering will. The result is a violent nature, rushing from one unbridled action to another.

A second deviation ensues when feeling is freed from normal restraint. A person inclined to revere others may then lapse into unlimited dependence, to the extent of losing all will and thought of his own. Instead of higher knowledge, the most pitiful vacuity and feebleness would be his lot. Or again, in these cases where feeling predominates, a person inclined to piety and devout exaltation can fall into transports of religious inebriation.

The third evil arises when thinking predominates, resulting in a contemplative nature hostile to life and enclosed within itself. For such people the world has importance only in so far as it provides them with objects for satisfying their boundless thirst for wisdom. No thought ever moves them to an action or a feeling. They are always cold and unsympathetic. They flee from every contact with everyday things as though it were abhorrent or at any rate had lost all meaning for them.

These are the three aberrations into which the pupil can stray: violence of will, sentimental emotionalism and cold, loveless striving for wisdom. For outward observation, and also from the standpoint of materialistic medicine, the picture of one who has thus gone astray is hardly distinguishable, above all in degree, from someone who is insane or at least suffering from severe nervous illness. Needless to say, the pupil must not come to resemble such people. It is essential for him that the three fundamental soul-forces, thinking, feeling and willing, should have undergone harmonious development before being released from their inherent connection and subordinated to the awakened higher consciousness. For once the mistake is made, if one of the soul-forces falls a prey to unbridled excess, the higher soul comes into evidence to begin with as a thing misborn. The unrestrained force then pervades the individual's whole personality and for a long time there can be no question of balance being restored. A predominance of thinking or feeling or willing, which would rank as a harmless characteristic in someone without esoteric training, is so intensified in the esoteric pupil as to obscure entirely the all-round human quality that is essential in daily life.

Admittedly, this does not become a really serious danger until the pupil has acquired the faculty of carrying into waking consciousness experiences that occur during sleep. So long as it is only a matter of illuminating the intervals of sleep, then the life of the senses, regulated by cosmic laws, reacts during waking hours on the disturbed equilibrium of the soul, restoring the balance. That is why it is so essential that the waking life of the pupil should be orderly and healthy in every respect. The more capable he is of meeting the demands made by the outer world upon a healthy, vigorous constitution of body, soul and spirit, the better it is for him. On the other hand it may be bad for him if his ordinary waking life has an exciting or irritating effect upon him—if, that is, any destructive or hampering influences affect his outer life in addition to the great changes taking place in his inner self. He should seek for everything, in keeping with his powers, that will bring him into undisturbed, harmonious communion with his environment. And he should avoid everything detrimental to this harmony—everything that brings unrest and feverish haste into his life. And here it is not so much a question of getting rid of this unrest and haste in an external sense, but far rather of taking care that the mood, the intentions, the thoughts and the bodily health are not exposed to continual fluctuations. None of this is as easy for the pupil during his esoteric training as it was before. For the higher experiences which now play into his life work uninterruptedly upon his whole existence. If anything in these higher experiences is not in order, the irregularity will be continually in wait for him and at every opportunity throw him off the right track. For this reason the pupil should neglect nothing that will ensure his mastery over his whole being. He should never be found wanting in presence of mind or fail to look calmly at all relevant situations in life. Fundamentally speaking, however, a genuine esoteric training gives rise of itself to all these qualities. As it progresses the pupil becomes acquainted with the dangers, while simultaneously and at the right moment acquiring full power to drive them from the field.

THE GUARDIAN OF THE
THRESHOLD

Important experiences during the pupil's ascent into the higher worlds are his meetings with the 'Guardian of the Threshold'. Strictly speaking there are two: a 'Lesser' and a 'Greater' Guardian. The pupil meets the Lesser Guardian when the threads connecting willing, feeling and thinking within the finer astral and etheric bodies begin to loosen in the way described in the last chapter. The Greater Guardian is encountered when this sundering of connections extends also to the physical parts of the body (primarily the brain).

The Lesser Guardian of the Threshold is an independent Being. He is not present for the pupil until the latter has reached the corresponding stage of development. Only some of the Guardian's most essential characteristics can here be indicated.

An attempt will now be made to present in narrative form the meeting with the Lesser Guardian of the Threshold. It is through this meeting that the pupil first becomes aware that his thinking, feeling and willing have freed themselves from the connections that have been implanted in them.

A truly terrible, spectral Being confronts the pupil, and he will need all that presence of mind and faith in the reliability of his path of knowledge which he has had ample opportunity to acquire in the course of his training.

The Guardian proclaims his significance in somewhat the following words:

'Hitherto, Powers invisible to yourself had charge of you. They saw to it that in the course of your life each of your good deeds had its reward and that each of your bad deeds was attended by its woeful consequences. Through the influence of these Powers your character formed itself out of your experiences and thoughts. They were the authors of your destiny. They determined the measure of joy and pain apportioned to you in your incarnations, according to your conduct. Their sovereignty over you took the form of the all-embracing law of Karma. These Powers will now partially remove their restraining influence, and you must now yourself accomplish some of the work which they have hitherto performed for you. Fate has struck you many a hard blow. You did not know why. It was the consequence of a harmful deed in one of your previous lives. You found happiness and joy and took them as they came. They, too, were the result of earlier deeds. In your character there are many fine sides and many ugly flaws. You have yourself caused both through previous experiences and thoughts. These were, until now, unknown to you; their effects alone were made manifest to you. But they, the Lords of Karma, beheld all your deeds in former lives, your most secret thoughts and feelings. And they determined accordingly what you now are and the manner of your present life.

'Now all the good and all the bad aspects of your bygone lives are to be revealed to you. Until now they were woven into your own being; they were within you and you could not see them, even as with physical eyes you cannot see your own brain. But now these aspects release themselves from you; they emerge from your personality. They assume an independent form which you can see, just as you see the stones and plants of the outer world. And I . . . am that very Being who has formed a body out of your noble and ignoble doings. My spectral form is woven out of the entries in the ledger of your life. Until now you have borne me invisibly within yourself. But it was well for you that this should be; for the wisdom of your destiny, though hidden from you, has thus also worked within you to eliminate the hideous flaws in my form. Now that I have come out of you, that hidden wisdom too has departed from you. Henceforth it will pay no further heed to you; it will leave the work in your hands alone. I must become a perfect and splendid Being in myself if I am not to fall prey to corruption; and if that were to happen I should drag you too down with me into a dark, corrupted world. If you would avoid this, then your own wisdom must become great enough to take over the task of that other, hidden wisdom which has departed from you. When you have crossed my Threshold I shall never for an instant leave your side as a form visible to you. And in future, whenever you act or think wrongly, you will immediately perceive your guilt as a hideous, demoniacal distortion of my form. Only when you have made good all your past misdeeds and have so purified yourself that all further evil is impossible for you, only then will my being be transformed into radiant beauty. Then, too, I shall again be able to unite with you for the blessing of your future activity.

'My Threshold is built out of every feeling of fear remaining in you, out of every shrinking from the power to assume full responsibility for all your deeds and thoughts. As long as you still have any trace of fear of becoming the director of your own destiny, for just so long does this Threshold lack something that must be built into it. And as long as a single stone is found missing you must remain at a standstill on this Threshold, as though transfixed; or else you must stumble. Do not, then, attempt to cross this Threshold until you feel entirely free from fear and ready for the highest responsibility.

'Hitherto I emerged from your own personality only when death recalled you from an earthly life; but even then my form was veiled from you. The Powers of Destiny who ruled over you, they alone beheld me, and in the intervals between death and a new birth developed in you, in accordance with the appearance I presented, the power and capacity wherewith in a new earthly life you could work at the beautifying of my form in order to ensure your progress. It was I, too, whose imperfection ever and again constrained the Powers of Destiny to lead you back to a new incarnation on the Earth. I was present at the hour of your death and it was for my sake that the Lords of Karma ordained your rebirth. Only by thus unconsciously transforming me to perfection through ever-recurring earthly lives could you have escaped the Powers of Death and passed into immortality united with me.

'Visible do I thus stand before you today, as I have ever stood invisible beside you in the hour of death. When you have crossed my Threshold you will enter those kingdoms to which otherwise you had access only after physical death. You now enter them with full knowledge, and henceforth as you move, outwardly visible, about the Earth, you will at the same time move in the kingdom of death; which is also the kingdom of eternal life. I am indeed the Angel of Death, but I am at the same time the bringer of a higher, inexhaustible life. Through me you will die while still living in the body, in order to be reborn into indestructible existence.

'The realm you are now entering will acquaint you with beings of a supersensible nature, and blessedness will be your lot. But I myself must provide your first acquaintanceship with that world; I who am your own creation. Formerly I lived upon your own life; but now, through you, I have awakened to an existence of my own and stand before you as the visible standard of your future deeds, perhaps also as your constant reproach. You have been able to create me but by so doing you have also undertaken the duty of transforming me.'

What is here indicated in narrative form must not be thought of as an allegory, but as an experience of the highest possible reality undergone by the esoteric student.*

The Guardian will warn him not to go further if he does not feel in himself the strength to fulfil the demands contained in the preceding discourse. However terrible the form assumed by the Guardian, it is only the effect of the pupil's past life, only his own character awakened into independent existence outside himself. This awakening is brought about by the separation of willing, thinking and feeling. To feel for the first time that one has oneself called

* It will be clear from the above that the 'Guardian of the Threshold' is an astral figure, revealed to the awakening higher vision of the esoteric pupil; and Spiritual Science leads to this supersensible meeting. To make the Guardian of the Threshold physically visible also is an operation connected with lower magic. It was done by producing a cloud of fine substance, a sort of smoke composed of a particular mixture of a number of substances. The developed power of the magician is then able to mould the cloud into form and to vitalise its substance with the still unredeemed karma of the individual concerned. Anyone who is adequately prepared for higher vision no longer needs a physical phenomenon of this kind; and anyone who with insufficient preparation sees his unredeemed karma appear as a living entity before his eyes is in danger of falling into evil byways. He should not strive for this result. In Bulwer Lytton's novel, *Zanoni* a description of this 'Guardian of the Threshold' is given in fictional form.

a spiritual Being into existence is in itself a profoundly significant experience. The aim of the pupil's preparation must be to enable him to endure the terrible sight without a trace of timidity, and at the moment of the meeting to feel his strength so increased that he can consciously undertake to make himself responsible for the ennoblement of the Guardian.

If successfully endured, this meeting with the Guardian of the Threshold results in the next physical death of the pupil being an event entirely different from previous deaths. He experiences consciously the process of dying, in that he lays aside the physical body as a garment that is worn out or has perhaps become useless because of a sudden rent. This physical death is then of consequence only for other people who live with him and whose perceptions are still restricted to the world of the senses. For them, the pupil 'dies'; but for him nothing of importance is changed in his whole environment. The whole supersensible world was open to him before his death, and after death this same world will lie open before him.

Now the Guardian of the Threshold is connected also with another matter. The individual concerned belongs to a family, to a people, to a race; his activity in the physical world depends upon his relationship to this kind of community. His particular character is also connected with it. The conscious activity of single individuals by no means exhausts everything to be reckoned with in a family, a people, or a race. As well as their characters, families, peoples and races also have their destinies. For persons restricted to their senses, these concepts are merely *generalisations* and the materialistic thinker, with his preconceptions, will look down contemptuously on the spiritual scientist when he hears that, for the latter, family or national characters, lineal or racial destinies are real Beings, as real as the personality produced by the character and destiny of an individual. The spiritual scientist learns to know higher worlds, of which the single personalities are members, just as arms and legs and heads are members of the human being. Besides the single individuals, the very real family-souls, folk-souls, race-spirits, are at work in the life of a family, a people, a race. Indeed in a certain sense the single individuals are only the executive organs of these family-souls, folk-souls, race-spirits, and so on. In all truth it can be said that a folk-soul, for example, makes use of each individual belonging to that people or folk for the execution of certain tasks. The folk-soul does not descend to physical reality but dwells in higher worlds, and in order to work in the physical world makes use of the physical organs of each individual. In a higher sense it is as when an architect makes use of workmen for executing the details of a building. In the truest sense every individual receives his allotted task from his family-, folk-, or race-soul.

Now the physical man is by no means informed about the higher purpose of his work. He works *unconsciously* at the aims of his people, of his race, and so forth. From the moment when the pupil meets the Guardian of the Threshold he is required not merely to know his own tasks as a personality, but to work with *conscious understanding* at those of his people or his race. Every extension of his horizon enlarges the scope of his duties. What actually happens is that the pupil adds a new body to his finer soul-body. He puts on another garment. Hitherto he has made his way through the world with the sheaths enveloping his personality; and what he had to accomplish for his community, his people, his race and so on was looked after by higher Spirits who made use of his personality.

A further revelation now made to the pupil by the Guardian of the Threshold is that henceforth these Spirits will withdraw their guiding hands from him. He must step right out of his community. And as an isolated individual he would become rigidly hardened within himself, he would head for destruction. if he did not himself acquire the powers which are inherent in the folk—and race-Spirits.

Many people no doubt, will say: 'Oh, I have freed myself entirely from all lineal and racial connections; I want to be simply a human being and nothing else.' But to these people one must reply: 'Who, then, brought you to this freedom? Was it not your family who placed you in your present position in the world? Have not your lineage, your people, your race, made you what you are? They have brought you up; and if now, raised above all prejudices, you are one of the lightbringers and benefactors of your stock or even of your race, it is to *their* upbringing that you owe it. Yes, even when you say you are "simply a human being", you owe what you have become to the Spirits of your communities.' The esoteric pupil alone learns what it means to be entirely cut off from his family, lineal or racial Spirits. He alone realises, through personal experience, the insignificance of all such upbringing for the life now confronting him. For everything inculcated into him dissolves completely when the threads binding willing, thinking and feeling are severed. He looks back on the results of all previous upbringing as he would look at a house crumbling away brick by brick, which he must now rebuild in a new form.

Again, it is more than a mere figure of speech to say that when the Guardian has uttered his first demands there arises from the place where he stands a whirlwind which extinguishes all the spiritual lights that have hitherto illumined the path of life. Utter darkness, broken only by the radiance streaming from the Guardian himself, stretches before the pupil. And out of this darkness resounds the Guardian's further admonitions: 'Step not across my Threshold before you realise that you must yourself illumine the darkness ahead of you; take not a single step forward until you are certain that you have enough oil in your own lamp. The lamps of those who were hitherto your Guides will in future not be available for you.' After these words the pupil must turn and direct his gaze backwards. The Guardian of the Threshold now draws aside a veil which hitherto had concealed deep mysteries of life.

The family-, folk- and race-Spirits are revealed in their full reality, so that the pupil sees clearly how he has been led up to now, and no less clearly that he will henceforth no longer have this guidance. That is the second warning received at the Threshold from its Guardian.

Without preparation, certainly, no one could endure the vista indicated here. But the higher training which makes it possible for the pupil to advance to the Threshold, at the same time equips him to find the necessary strength at the right moment. Indeed, the training can have such a harmonious effect that the entry into the new life is freed from any agitating or tumultuous effects. The pupil's experience at the Threshold will then be accompanied by a foretaste of the blessedness that is to be the keynote of his newly awakened life. Awareness of the new freedom will outweigh all other feelings; and his new duties and new responsibilities will appear as something which man, at a certain stage of life, must take upon himself.

LIFE AND DEATH. THE GREAT
GUARDIAN OF THE THRESHOLD

The significance for an individual of the meeting with the so-called Lesser Guardian of the Threshold has been described by showing that in this figure he becomes aware of a supersensible Being he has himself brought into existence, and whose body is made up of the consequences —hitherto invisible to him—of his own acts, feelings and thoughts. But these unseen forces have become the cause of his destiny and his character and he realises how he himself laid down in the past the foundations of his present existence. His essential being now stands to a certain extent openly revealed before him. He has, for example, certain definite inclinations and habits. Now he can recognise why he has them, and what was the origin of certain blows of fate that befell him. He sees why he loves one thing and hates another; why one thing delights him and another saddens him. Visible life becomes intelligible to him through the invisible causes. The essential facts of life, health and illness, death and birth, unveil themselves before his sight. He observes how *before* his birth he wove the causes which led him back into life. Henceforth he knows the being within himself who has been imperfectly developed in this visible world and can be brought to final fulfilment *only* in this same visible world. For in no other world is there any opportunity for working at the development of this being. Furthermore he realises that death cannot sever him for ever from this world. He says to himself: 'I once came into this world for the first time because then I was a being who needed the life it provided in order to acquire attributes unattainable in any other world. And I must remain bound to this world until I have developed within myself everything to be gained there. I shall one day become a useful fellow-worker in another world only by having acquired all the faculties for it in this physical, visible world.'

One of the most significant experiences of the Initiate is that he gains a better knowledge and appreciation of the true value of physically visible Nature than was possible before his spiritual training. This knowledge comes to him precisely through his insight into the supersensible world. Anyone not possessing this insight, and perhaps vaguely imagining that the supersensible regions are infinitely the more valuable, may underestimate the physical world. But one who has this insight knows that without his experiences in the visible reality he would be utterly powerless in the invisible reality. If he is to *live* in the latter, he must have faculties and instruments for so doing; and these he can acquire only in the visible world. If the invisible world is to become a conscious experience for him, he must be capable of spiritual *sight*. But this power of vision in a 'higher' world is developed gradually through experiences in the 'lower'. One can no more be born in a spiritual world with spiritual eyes, if they have not been developed in the physical world, than a child could be born with physical eyes if they had not already been formed within the mother's body.

From this standpoint it will be readily understood why the 'Threshold' to the supersensible world is watched by a 'Guardian'. In no case may real insight into those regions be permitted to anyone before he has acquired the necessary faculties; therefore at each death, if a man who is still incapable of working in another world enters that world, its experiences are shrouded from him. He may behold them only when he has become completely ripe for them.

When the pupil enters the supersensible world, life acquires an entirely new meaning for him; he discerns in the physical world the seed-ground of a higher world. And in a certain sense this 'higher' world will appear defective without the 'lower'. Two vistas open out before him: one into the past, the other into the future. He looks into a past when this physical world did not yet exist; for he has long since outgrown the preconception that the super-sensible world evolved out of the sense-world. He knows that the supersensible world existed first, and that everything physical evolved out of it. He sees that he himself belonged to a supersensible world *before* coming for the first time into this sense-world. But this pristine supersensible world needed to pass through the sense-world; otherwise its further evolution would not have been possible. The supersensible beings can resume their progress only when certain other beings have developed appropriate faculties in the phenomenal world. And these other beings are *men*. As they now are, with their present mode of life, they have sprung from an imperfect stage of spiritual existence and are being led, even within this stage, towards that fulfilment which will make them fit for further work in the higher world. And here a view into the future opens out. It points towards a higher stage of the supersensible world—a stage that will be enriched with fruits brought to maturity in the sense-world. The sense-world as such will be overcome; but its results will be incorporated into a higher world.

Disease and death in the sense-world are thus explained. Death is nothing else than an expression of the fact that the supersensible world, as it once was, reached a point from which it could not progress by itself. Universal death would inevitably have overtaken it if it had not received a new influx of life. And this new life has become a battle against universal death. Out of the remnants of a dying, inwardly rigidifying world the seeds of a new world came to flower. That is why we have death and life in the world. The dying parts of the old world still cling to the seeds of the new life, which were indeed their offspring. This comes to expression most clearly of all in man himself. He bears as his sheath what has been preserved from that old world, and within this sheath is formed the seed of the being who will live in the future.

Thus man is a twofold being: mortal and immortal.

The mortal being is in its last stage, the immortal being in its initial stage. But it is only *within* this twofold world, which finds its expression in the physical world of sense, that he can acquire the requisite faculties to lead the world on to immortality. Indeed, his task is precisely to gather from the mortal world itself the fruits for the immortal. When he contemplates his own being and nature, which he himself has produced in the past, he cannot but say to himself: 'I have in me the elements of a dying world. They are at work in me and I can only gradually break their power through the newly arising elements of immortality.' Thus does man's path lead from death to life. Could he commune with himself in the hour of death, he would say: 'The dying world was my teacher. That I am dying is a result of the whole past with which I am interwoven. But the field of mortality has brought to maturity within me the seeds of immortality. I bear these seeds with me into another world. If it depended only on the past, I could never have been born. The life of the past came to an end with birth. Life in the sense-world is wrested from universal death by the newly formed seed of life. The time between birth and death is only the expression of how much the new life could wrest from the dying past. And illness is nothing but the continuing effect of the dying parts of the past.'

From all this the answer is found to the question why man only gradually works his way through error and imperfection to the true and the good. His deeds, feelings and thoughts are, to begin with, under the sway of the perishable and mortal. Out of the latter his physical sense-organs were formed. Hence these organs and everything that at first urges them on are doomed to perish. The imperishable will not be found in the instincts, impulses, passions and the organs belonging to them, but only in what these organs accomplish. Only when man has drawn out from the perishable everything it can yield, will he be able to cast away the foundations out of which he has grown and which find their expression in the physical world of the senses.

Thus the first Guardian of the Threshold comes before the individual as a replica of his twofold nature, a blend of the perishable and the imperishable. And the figure of the Guardian shows clearly how it falls short of that sublime form of Light which can dwell again in the world of pure spirit.

The extent to which the individual is entangled in the physical world of the senses is made concretely perceptible through the Guardian of the Threshold. The presence of instincts, impulses, desires, egotistical wishes, all forms of selfishness and so forth are evidence of this entanglement; it is expressed also in his membership of a race, a people, and so forth. For peoples and races are only different stages of evolution on the way to pure manhood. A race or a people stands at a higher level in proportion as its members bring to expression the pure, ideal type of manhood, and in so far as they have worked their way from the physcial

207

and perishable to the supersensible and imperishable. The evolution of man through reincarnations in ever higher ethnic and racial forms is thus a process of liberation. Man must ultimately appear in his harmonious perfection. In a similar way, the pilgrimage through ever purer forms of morality and religion is a perfecting process; for every stage of morality still harbours a yearning for the perishable as well as the seeds of an ideal future.

Now in the Guardian of the Threshold, as described above, the product of the past alone is made manifest, containing only such seeds of the future as were woven into it in this past time. But the individual must take with him into the future supersensible world everything he can draw from the world of the senses. If he were to bring with him only what has been woven into his counterpart out of the past, his earthly task would have been only partly accomplished. For this reason the Lesser Guardian of the Threshold is joined, after a time, by the Greater Guardian. The meeting with this second Guardian of the Threshold will again be described in narrative form.

When the pupil has recognised the things from which he must free himself, an exalted Being of Light stands before him on his path. The beauty of this Being is difficult to describe in human language. This meeting takes place when the organs of thinking, feeling and willing have so far freed themselves from each other, in relation even to the physical body, that their reciprocal connection is no longer regulated by themselves but by the higher consciousness that is now entirely liberated from physical conditions. The organs of thinking, feeling and willing have then become instruments under the sway of the human soul, which exercises its dominion over them from supersensible regions. The soul, thus liberated from all bonds of the senses, is now confronted by the second Guardian of the Threshold, who speaks to somewhat the following effect:

'You have released yourself from the world of the senses. Your right to a home in the supersensible world has been won. You can now work from out of this world. For your own part you no longer require your physical bodily nature in its present form. If your intention was merely to acquire the capacity to dwell in this supersensible world, you need no longer return to the sense-world. But now, gaze on me. See how immeasurably I am raised above all that you have made of yourself until now. You have attained your present degree of perfection through the faculties you were able to develop in the sense-world as long as you were still dependent upon it. But now there must begin for you an era when your liberated powers will work further in the world of the senses. Hitherto you have only realised yourself, but now, having yourself become free, you can liberate all your companions in the sense-world. Until today you have striven as an individual; now make yourself a member of the whole, so that you may bring into the supersensible world not yourself alone, but everything else that exists in the world of the senses. You will some day be able to unite yourself with me, but I cannot find blessedness as long as others are still unredeemed! As a liberated individual you might enter this very day into the supersensible world, but then you would be obliged to look down on the still unredeemed beings in the sense-world; you would have separated your destiny from theirs. But you are all linked together; you had all to descend into the sense-world in order to gather from it powers needed for the higher world. Were you to separate yourself from the others, you would be misusing the powers you have been able to develop only in association with them. If they had not descended, you could not have done so; without them the powers needed for your supersensible existence would be lacking. You must now share with the others the powers you acquired in their company. I therefore forbid you admission into the highest regions of the supersensible world as long as you have not applied to the redemption of the world to which you belong all the powers you have acquired. With the powers you have already achieved you may sojourn in the lower regions of the supersensible world; but before the portal of the higher I stand (as the Cherubin with the fiery sword before Paradise), and I forbid your entrance as long as you retain powers that have not been put to use in the sense-world. And if you will not apply your powers in this way, others coming later will apply them. Then a higher supersensible world will receive all the fruits of the sense-world, but the ground in which you were rooted will be withdrawn from you. The purified world will evolve above and beyond you. You will be excluded from it. Then you would be treading the *black* path, while those from whom you have separated yourself would be treading the *white* path.'

The 'Great Guardian' of the Threshold thus announces his presence soon after the meeting with the first Watcher has taken place. But the Initiate knows full well what is in store for him if he yields to the temptations of a premature sojourn in the supersensible world. An indescribable splendour radiates from the second Guardian; union with him lies as a far distant ideal before the eye of the soul. Yet there is also the certainty that this union will not be possible until all the powers which have come to the Initiate from this world are applied by him to liberating and redeeming this world. If he resolves to fulfil the demands of the higher Being of Light, the Initiate will be able to contribute to the liberation of the human race. He brings his gifts to the altar of humanity. If he gives preference to his own premature elevation into the supersensible world, the stream of human evolution will pass him by. After his liberation he can acquire no new powers for himself from the sense-world. If he nevertheless places his achievements at the disposal of the sense-world, he has to renounce all prospect of gaining anything more for himself from the scene of his future work.

It does not follow that when called upon to make the decision, a man will obviously choose the white path. This depends entirely upon whether at the time of the decision he is already so far purified that no trace of self-seeking makes the allurements of blessedness appear desirable. These allurements are the strongest imaginable; whereas on the other side no special allurements are evident. Here, nothing appeals to egoism, What the individual will receive in the higher regions of the supersensible world is nothing that comes to him, but entirely something that goes out from him: love for the world and for his fellows. Nothing that egoism desired is denied upon the black path. On the contrary: the fruits of this path are the complete gratification of egoism. And if anyone desires blessedness for himself alone he will certainly tread the black path, for it is the appropriate one for him. No one, therefore, should expect that the occultists of the white path will give him instruction for the development of his own egotistical self. They have not the slightest interest in the blessedness of the individual. Everyone can attain that for himself. It is not the task of the white occultists to accelerate that achievement. They are concerned entirely with the development and liberation of all beings—men and the companions of men. Therefore the instructions they give deal only with how man can develop his powers for co-operating in this work. Hence they value devotion and readiness for sacrifice above all other attributes. They never actually reject anyone, for even the greatest egotist can purify himself. But as long as anyone is seeking some advantage for himself alone he will get nothing from the occultists. Even when they do not withdraw their help from him, he deprives himself of its fruits. Therefore one who genuinely follows the instructions of the good occult teachers will, after crossing the Threshold, understand the demands of the Great Guardian; one who does not follow the instructions given by these teachers cannot possibly hope to reach the Threshold through their guidance. Their instructions lead to the good —or to nothing at all. It is no part of their task to lead to egoistic blessedness and to mere existence in the super-sensible world. From the very outset it lies in the nature of their task to keep the pupil away from the supersensible world until he can enter it with the will for selfless co-operation.

APPENDIX
to the 8th edition, Berlin, 1918

The path to supersensible knowledge described in this book leads to experiences in the life of soul concerning which it is of the utmost importance that the pupil should be under no illusions or misunderstandings. It is quite easy for anyone to deceive himself about these things. One of the most serious illusions arises when the whole range of inner experience spoken of in true Spiritual Science is so distorted that it appears to come into the same category as superstition, visionary dreaming, mediumship and many other degenerate pursuits. The reason often is that persons who fall into these undersirable ways through searching for supersensible reality by methods alien to a genuine striving for knowledge are confused with those who desire to follow the path described in this book. The experiences lived through by the human soul on this path belong entirely to the realm of soul and spirit. Such experiences are open only to a person for whom they have become as freely independent of his bodily life as are, in ordinary consciousness, the thoughts we form about the objects of our perceiving, feeling and willing, thoughts not engendered by these objects themselves. There are people who do not believe that such thoughts exist. Their contention is that a man can have no thoughts not drawn from perceptions or from an inner life conditioned by the body. For these people all thoughts are, as it were, shadow-images of perceptions or of inner experiences. Anyone who makes such a statement does so only because he has never developed the faculty of experiencing in his soul the self-sustaining life of pure thought. For those who have lived through this experience it has become a matter of actual knowledge that wherever *thinking* holds sway in the life of soul, then, in so far as this thinking permeates other functions of the soul, a person is engaged in an activity wherein his body plays no part. In the ordinary life of the soul, thinking is almost always mingled with other functions: perception, feeling, willing, and so forth. These other functions are engendered by the body, but thinking plays into them, and to the extent to which this happens, something takes place in and through the human being wherein the body has no share. People who deny this are prisoners of the illusion caused by the fact that they always observe the activity of thinking united with other functions. But through inward endeavour one can come to experience this thinking activity in itself, separated from the rest of the inner life. Something consisting only of pure thoughts can be detached from the compass of soul-life—thoughts which are self-sustaining and from which everything provided by perception or by bodily conditioned inner life is eliminated. Such thoughts reveal themselves through themselves, through what they are, as spiritual, supersensible reality. And the soul that unites with them, excluding during the union all perception, all memory and all other forms of inner life, knows itself, in the activity of thinking, to be in a supersensible region, outside the physical body. For anyone cognisant of this whole process the question whether the soul can experience itself in a supersensible element outside the body simply does not arise. For this would mean denying what he knows from actual experience. The only question for him is: what is it that prevents people from recognising such an irrefutable fact? And the answer he finds is that this reality does not reveal itself if the individual has not previously cultivated a condition of soul which will enable him to receive this revelation.

Now to begin with people become distrustful if an activity purely of the nature of soul is necessary on their part in order that something essentially independent of them may be revealed. They believe that it is they themselves who give the revelation its content because they have to prepare themselves before being able to receive it. They want to have experiences to which they contribute nothing and which allow them to remain quite passive. If such people are also ignorant of the most elementary requirements for a scientific grasp of a given fact, they will take as an objective revelation of *non*-material reality, the contents and products of soul-life in cases where the soul has been allowed to fall below the degree of conscious activity displayed in sense-perception and deliberate action. Visionary experiences and mediumistic phenomena are examples of this. But what comes to light through revelations of this character is not a supersensible but a subsensible world. Man's conscious waking life does not take its course wholly within the body; the conscious part of it takes its course above all at the boundary between the body and the physical outer world. Hence the process of perception in the sense-organs is as much the penetration of an extra-bodily process *into* the body as a 'permeation' proceeding *from* the body. And so, too, is the life of will, which depends upon man being embedded in cosmic existence, so that what happens in him through his will is simultaneously part of happenings in the world. In this life of soul at the boundary of the body, man is to a high degree dependent on his bodily organisation; but the activity of thinking plays into this experience, and in so far as it does so, man makes himself independent of his bodily organisation in acts of sense-perception and willing. In visionary experience and mediumistic demonstrations, man becomes wholly dependent on his body. He excludes from his life of soul the very activity which in acts of perception and willing makes him independent of his body. Thus the contents and products of his soul are then merely revelations of his bodily life. Visionary experiences and demonstrations of mediumship spring from the circumstance that the individual, while in this condition, is in his soul less independent of his body than in the ordinary life of perception and will. In the experience of the supersensible indicated in this book, the development of soul-life proceeds in the opposite direction from that of visionary and mediumistic experience. The soul makes itself progressively more independent of the body than it is in the life of perception and will. Through experiencing pure thoughts, it achieves an independence which then extends over a much wider range of soul-activities.

For the supersensible activity here meant, it is exceptionally important to have a clear understanding of the experience of pure thinking. Fundamentally speaking, this experience itself is already a supersensible activity of the soul, only it is one in which nothing supersensible is yet perceived. With pure thinking one lives in the supersensible, but one experiences *this* alone in a supersensible way; one does not, as yet, experience anything else of a supersensible nature. And supersensible experience must be a continuation of that experience in the life of soul which can be attained in union with pure thinking. Hence it is so important to understand this union rightly. For from understanding of this union shines the light that can bring true insight into the nature of supersensible knowledge. If the soul's experience were to sink below the level of clear consciousness maintained in thinking, the soul would immediately be on the wrong path as far as true knowledge of the supersensible world is concerned. It would be laid hold of by the bodily functions, and what it experiences and brings to light is then not a revelation of the supersensible, but a revelation of bodily activity in the sub-sensory world.

As soon as the soul penetrates into the domain of the

supersensible, its experiences are of such a nature that linguistic expressions cannot so easily be found for them as for experiences in the world of the senses. In descriptions of supersensible experiences one must often be particularly conscious that the gulf separating the actual facts from the language used is greater than with physical experience. It must be understood that many an expresison is like a pictorial representation, merely indicating in a delicate way the reality to which it refers. Thus it is said on page 32 of this book that originally all the rules and teachings of Spiritual Science were expressed in a symbolic sign-language. And on page 80 a certain writing-system or 'script' was spoken of. Now someone may easily be led to suppose that such a script can be learnt in the way that the letters and their combinations in an ordinary physical language can be learnt. In this connection it must be said that there have been and still are esoteric schools and associations in the possession of symbolic signs by means of which they bring supersensible facts to expression. And one who is initiated into the meaning of these symbols has thereby a means of directing his inner experiences to the supersensible realities in question. But it is much more important that in the course of the supersensible experience which the soul can reach by making a reality of the contents of this book, the soul should come to a revelation of the script through its own contemplation of the supersensible. The supersensible says something to the soul which the soul must translate into pictorial signs in order to be able to survey it in full consciousness. It may be said that what is communicated in this script *can* be confirmed by every soul. And in the course of this confirmation, which the soul can itself regulate in accordance with the indications given, the results that have been described become evident. A book such as this should be taken as a conversation between the author and the reader. When it is said that the pupil needs personal instruction, this should be understood in the sense that the book itself is personal instruction. In earlier times there were reasons for confining personal instructions to oral esoteric teaching; today we have reached a stage in the evolution of mankind when spiritual-scientific knowledge must spread far more widely than before. It must be accessible to everyone to an extent quite different from what was the rule in bygone times. So the book takes the place of the former oral teaching. The belief that further personal instruction is necessary, over and above what is contained in this book is true only in a qualified sense. No doubt someone may need personal assistance and this may be of greater importance for him; but it would be erroneous to believe that there are any cardinal matters not mentioned in the book. They can be found by those who read correctly, and, above all, *completely*.

The descriptive instructions given in this book may seem to call for a complete transformation of the entire man. But when they are rightly read it will be found that the intention is simply to indicate the inner disposition of soul required by a man in those moments of his life when he desires to confront the supersensible world. He develops this disposition of soul as a second being within himself; and his other healthy being pursues its course as before. He knows how to hold the two beings apart in full consciousness and how to establish the right interaction between them. He does not become useless and incompetent in life through losing interest and skill in it, being 'taken up with spiritual investigation all day long'. It is of course true that the pupil's mode of experience in the supersensible world will shed light over his whole being; but far from distracting him from life, it makes him more capable and his life more productive. The reason why the descriptions given here have to be used is because every cognitive process directed towards the supersensible calls the entire human being into action. Whereas in the process of perceiving colour, the eye alone, with its adjoining nervous system is engaged, the process of supersensible cognition engages the *whole* man. The man becomes 'all eye' or 'all ear'. When, therefore, information concerning the processes of supersensible cognition is given, it appears as though a transformation of the human being were meant; as if nothing were right in the ordinary human being and he should become quite different.

I should like to add something to what has been said from page 117 onwards concerning 'Some Effects of

Initiation'; with slight modification it holds good also for other sections of this book. Someone might well be struck by the thought: what is the purpose of pictorial illustrations of supersensible experience? Could not this experience be described in ideas without such pictures? The answer must be that for the experience of supersensible reality it is essential that the individual should know himself to be a supersensible being in a supersensible world. Without this perception of his own supersensible being, whose reality is fully revealed, in its own way, in the descriptions here given of the 'lotus-flowers' and the 'etheric body', the individual's experience of himself in the supersensible world would be as though he were placed in the material world in such a way that the things and happenings around him were apparent to him, while he had no knowledge of his own body. His perception of his own supersensible form in 'soul-body' and 'etheric body' enables him to stand, conscious of himself, in the supersensible world, just as he is conscious of himself in the physical world through the perception of his physical body.

List of relevant literature (published, except where otherwise stated, by Rudolf Steiner Press)

By Rudolf Steiner:
Occult Science—an Outline
Theosophy. An Introduction to the supersensible Knowledge of the World and the Destination of Man
A Road to Self-Knowledge in Eight Meditations
The Threshold of the Spiritual World
Stages of Higher Knowledge
Practical Training in Thinking
Verses and Meditations

Lecture Courses:
The Theosophy of the Rosicrucian
Anthroposophy: an Introduction
The Evolution of Consciousness
True and False Paths in Spiritual Investigation

On the life and work of Rudolf Steiner:
A Scientist of the Invisible. By A. P. Shepherd (Hodder & Stoughton)

All the published works of Rudolf Steiner in German and in English translation, as well as those by other authors on related subjects, can be obtained from:

Rudolf Steiner Press
35 Park Road
London, N.W.1

Catalogues are available.

COMPLETE EDITION

of the works of Rudolf Steiner in the original German. Published by the *Rudolf Steiner Nachlassverwaltung, Dornach, Switzerland*, by whom all rights are reserved.

General Plan (abbreviated):

A. WRITINGS

I. Works written between the years 1883 and 1925
II. Essays and articles written between 1882 and 1925
III. Letters, drafts, manuscripts, fragments, verses, inscriptions, meditative sayings, etc.

B. LECTURES

I. Public Lectures
II. Lectures to Members of the Anthroposophical Society on general anthroposophical subjects
    Lectures to Members on the history of the Anthroposophical Movement and Anthroposophical Society
III. Lectures and Courses on special branches of work:
    Art: Eurythmy, Speech and Drama, Music, Visual Arts, History of Art
    Education
    Medicine and Therapy
    Science
    Sociology and the Threefold Social Order
    Lectures given to Workmen at the Goetheanum

The total number of lectures amounts to some six thousand, shorthand reports of which are available in the case of the great majority.

C. REPRODUCTIONS and SKETCHES

Paintings in water colours, drawings, coloured diagrams, Eurythmy forms, etc.

When the edition is complete the total number of volumes, each of a considerable size, will amount to several hundreds. A full and detailed *Bibliographical Survey*, with subjects, dates and places where the lectures were given, is available.

All the volumes can be obtained from the Rudolf Steiner Press in London as well as directly from the *Rudolf Steiner Nachlassverwaltung* (address as above).